The Art of
KNITTING HATS

30
Easy-to-Follow Patterns to Create
Your Own Colorwork Masterpieces

Courtney Flynn, Creator of flynnknit

PAGE STREET
PUBLISHING CO.

PAGE STREET
PUBLISHING CO.

First published in 2022 by
Page Street Publishing Co.
27 Congress Street, Suite 1511
Salem, MA 01970
www.pagestreetpublishing.com

Distributed by Macmillan, sales in Canada by The Canadian Manda Group.

26 25 24 23 22   2 3 4 5 6

ISBN-13: 978-1-64567-701-7
ISBN-10: 1-6456-7701-X

Library of Congress Control Number: 2022935245

Cover and book design by Molly Kate Young for Page Street Publishing Co.
Photography by Courtney Flynn and Memory Lanes Photography

Printed and bound in the United States of America

Dedication

For my parents, Doug and Elaine Challos, who instilled in me a love for the arts, nature and everything good in this world.

And for Holly Pritchard, who, without hesitation and with enthusiasm, shared the art of knitting with me. I don't think she had any idea what a profound impact her generosity would have—such an awesome reminder to always lift up others because you never know what one act of kindness will inspire or where it will lead.

Contents

INTRODUCTION

I am super excited you are here, my friends, and I'm thrilled to share my love for the art of knitting with you. I like to think of each piece that I create as its own little masterpiece, and my goal here is to help you see the same thing in your knits by letting the artist within you shine!

In this book, you will find hat patterns designed to get you started on your colorwork journey or, if you already have some experience, catapult you to the next level by experimenting with color combinations. Hats are the perfect outlet to really play with color because they are quick to make and not a major commitment. You start with a couple balls of yarn, and a few hours later, you have a finished piece! If you want, you can even make multiple versions of the same design using different colors, giving each piece its own unique vibe. I've always said that patience is a virtue . . . that I do not have. So, I love being able to knit up beautiful, artistic hats so quickly, and I hope you will, too!

I have designed a range of patterns within these pages so you can find plenty of choices that are right for you. As you make your way through the chapters in this book, you'll find that, for the most part, they start with beginner-friendly patterns and keep building on skills as you go. Each pattern also includes a skill level. Projects that use fewer colors and do not require you to catch long floats, for example, are marked as "Easy." Patterns that

include more advanced skills such as seaming a double brim are noted as "Intermediate." But no matter which pattern skill level you choose, you'll always find lots of helpful hints and chart notes. You'll also find easy tips and tricks—I always resort to easy, my friends, as I want to make the knitting process as simple for you as possible. I also want you to be able to knit my designs in multiple types of yarn, so you'll find recommended substitutions for each pattern. This way you can feel comfortable knitting my patterns whether you decide to use yarn from a major craft store or your favorite indie-dyed yarn from your local yarn shop.

And before we go much further, let me address the elephant in the room: color combinations. So often I hear knitters stress about yarn pairings when it comes to colorwork or say, "I could never put colors together like that!" Guess what? You totally can! And I'm here to help. I want the patterns you find here to inspire you to toss aside any inhibitions you might have about colorwork and embrace this opportunity to start considering your knits as art. Once you do this, so much of the worry about putting together the "perfect" color combination fades away because you'll be able to see the beauty in each of your creations. I want you to feel a sense of empowerment that every piece you create is its own masterpiece. And I hope you find inspiration in the color combinations I used for the patterns in this book.

I have been a lover of all forms of art since I was a kid. I remember getting super excited when I got a fresh box of crayons. I would pull out each one to learn its name and then grab a coloring book to start filling in the white space. Then, I got into drawing with colored pencils and markers, I explored paint by number, and later I played with abstract watercolor pieces. When I began knitting about six years ago, I felt like it was an extension of those early artforms I was drawn to when I was younger. It gave me another chance to "color" and to "paint," but this time I was using yarn as my medium and hats as my blank canvases.

I started out making basic scarves for everyone I knew and then ventured into hats. At some point, a friend encouraged me to start an Instagram account to share my knitting journey. I quickly became obsessed with knitting and photographing my knits as well. The more fun I had with it, the more I knew I needed to turn my passion into a business. That's how flynnknit was created.

I then began selling my finished hats on Etsy and in the gift shop of a local farm. My first order from the farm was about 40 hats. The next year the demand jumped to 100. Then, it grew to 200 each year. In the meantime, I also began experimenting with writing and self-publishing my own patterns.

My business really exploded as my Instagram photos featuring fun flat lays of my patterns in bold color combinations continued to gain more and more attention. I view the hats I create as art, and I love photographing them in artistic ways as well. I have knit hundreds of colorwork hats over the past few years; I never get tired of making them because there are endless color combinations, and I find so much joy and beauty in each new piece I create!

So, what are you feeling right now? Browse through these pages, find something you like, and tap into your inner artist. Don't look back. Are you thinking hot pink and neon yellow? Go with it! Or is your mood more neutral vibes with charcoal gray and cream? You can totally do that! Knit what speaks to you in the moment. And can I tell you something? There really is no wrong combination as long as you work with colors that have high contrast.

Now let's get to knitting and create some beautifully unique masterpieces!

♡ Courtney

COLORWORK BASICS

Before those needles start flying, I want to share some general information about colorwork with you! Definitely keep in mind that although there are some standard techniques, every knitter tends to have their own way of accomplishing them. I'll share some of my favorite tips and tricks with you, and you can choose what works best for you!

Choosing Colors and Yarn

When working a colorwork pattern, you use more than one color of yarn at a time. Picking the right color combination can be intimidating for some knitters, but I truly believe there is no wrong pairing as long as you pick colors with high contrast. Think eggplant purple and mustard yellow, or hot pink and a muted tan. You can even use very different shades of the same color—a dark, charcoal gray combined with a pale gray totally works! I apply this theory when I'm using three or more colors as well. I ask myself if there is high contrast at every point where the colors touch in the pattern. I find the easiest way to do this is to lay out the skeins I want to work with and move them around. I might place two next to each other for a bit and then move one color next to a different skein. Just play with them—this will help you visualize the contrast.

I tend to prefer solids or saturated tonals to help showcase the details of a design and make it pop. But I'm also obsessed with the beauty of variegated yarn, and you can totally use it as long as you're careful with your color pairing. If you're anything like me, you might tend to "match" a variegated yarn with a solid color. For example, if I'm using a variegated yarn with shades of blue and green, I immediately try to pair it with a solid green or blue to "match." You want to avoid doing this for colorwork because anytime the variegated yarn touches the solid in the pattern, the detail of the design can get lost. It's better to think about variegated yarn the same way you do when choosing solids—look for high contrast. Pair that blueish green variegated yarn with a solid orange yarn!

Another tip is to either use the same brand and type of yarn for all your colors in a project or use different brands of yarn that are super similar in thickness. Yarn can vary a lot even within the same weight category. One brand of bulky weight yarn may be on the thicker side, while a bulky style from another brand or dyer might be on the thinner side. If you try to mix yarns with different thicknesses in colorwork, the definition of your stitches can get lost because the thicker yarn tends to be more prominent. Again, it's totally okay to incorporate different brands of yarn within the same pattern, but just be mindful of the differences that exist and try to pick yarn that is as similar as possible. Once you choose the different colors you want to work with, I highly recommend you knit a swatch with them to determine how they work together. If you're happy with the swatch, go for it!

How to Read a Chart

I want to share with you the ins and outs of reading a chart; once you know the basics, you'll be good to go!

Think of a chart as a road map for knitting a hat. All the charts in this book are worked in the round, not back and forth, so the round will always start on the right-hand side of the chart, in the same way you knit stitches, using your right needle to move stitches off your left needle. In addition, all the hats in this book are knit from bottom to top (brim to crown). So when you read a chart, you also read it from bottom to top.

Each chart in this book features a color key next to it, indicating which color to use for each stitch you knit.

The chart represents how the knitting looks from the right side; it's a picture of the finished colorwork pattern as well as visual instructions. Each chart displays a section of the entire design that will be repeated in certain multiples. For example, if your chart contains 6 columns and you cast on 60 stitches, you will repeat each illustrated section 10 times before moving on to the next round. The specific number of repeats will be indicated in each pattern.

Work through each row of the chart starting in the bottom right corner and moving to the left from square to square. Each square on the chart represents one stitch in that color, and if there are no symbols in the square, that stitch is knit in that color. Once you reach the end of a row in the chart, you continue to repeat the same chart row from right to left until you reach the end of the round in your knitting. Then, move up to the next row. Again, starting on the right side of the chart for that row, work your way across the row to the left and repeat each section from right to left until you reach the end of the round. Continue to work the entire chart, moving up row by row, until you reach the top.

In the example below, I have included written instructions next to the chart just to help you get a better understanding of how to read it.

Example:

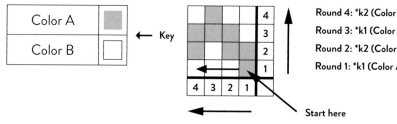

Round 4: *k2 (Color B), k1 (Color A), k1 (Color B); repeat from * to end.

Round 3: *k1 (Color B), k3 (Color A); repeat from * to end.

Round 2: *k2 (Color A), k1 (Color B), k1 (Color A); repeat from * to end.

Round 1: *k1 (Color A), k3 (Color B); repeat from * to end.

that gauge) will be listed for each pattern in this book, and it is important for you to match the gauge. Please note that all these gauges are for before blocking; because hats are relatively small projects, I find it easier to list gauge pre-blocking so you can check it as you knit.

Because tension (how tight or how loose your stitches are) varies from one knitter to the next, it is important to check your stitch count for the specified pattern gauge as you knit to make sure you're on track.

- If you count more stitches and more rounds within the specified gauge, your stitches are smaller than the gauge stitch size, and I would recommend increasing your needle size.

- If you count fewer stitches and fewer rounds within the specified gauge, your stitches are larger than the gauge stitch size, and I would recommend decreasing your needle size.

Gauge and Tension

Before I get into the details about gauge, let me start by saying that gauge is super important, my friends—like, *super* important to ensure you achieve the right size of any handknit piece. It can mean the difference between ending up with a hat that has a great fit or ending up with a tiny hat or a hat that is way too large.

Gauge is the size of stitches, and in these patterns, it is measured by the number of stitches per inch (2.5 cm) that are knit horizontally across your work and the number of rounds per inch (2.5 cm) that are knit vertically. Oftentimes, gauge is listed within a defined area such as a 4-inch (10-cm) square. A specific gauge (and suggested needle size to achieve

How to Hold Your Yarn

There are a variety of ways that knitters hold their yarn while knitting colorwork, and it really comes down to what feels most comfortable for you. You might hold both strands of yarn that you are working with in your right hand. Or you might hold them both in your left. Maybe you hold one strand of yarn in each hand as you knit. Or, if you're like me, you pick up and drop each strand of yarn as you work with it.

Whatever way works best for you, it is important to always try to keep your tension as similar as possible between colors and to not pull one color tighter than the other.

Yarn Position/Dominance

When knitting colorwork, it is important to always pull your colors from the same position while knitting to keep your stitches and floats nice and tidy.

When I work with two colors in one round, I keep the first color I'm using to the right of me and always pull it over the other color from the top position. I keep the other color I'm using to the left of me and always pull it from under the first color.

Some knitters believe that if you always pull your yarn from the same position and change the color you are working with, one color will tend to be more dominant and result in slightly larger stitches. This will give the appearance of one color popping out of the design more than the other.

Usually, when a pattern color is held to the left of the background color, this makes it dominant, but this can be affected by individual ways of tensioning and knitting technique and isn't always a rule. The basic principle is that the color traveling the longest distance to the working position uses more yarn and produces a larger stitch. This makes it appear more prominent, and it is considered the dominant color. For your pattern color to be dominant, make sure the floats in that color strand under the background color, and the background color strands over the pattern color.

If you find this is what happens when you knit, and you want one color to dominate the other, be very consistent in how you hold your colors and change colors. Assign one position to the pattern color and one to the background color, and always move them to the working position from the same direction, making sure the dominant color is traveling farther than the non-dominant color.

Other knitters believe that tension plays more of a role and that if you keep the same tension while knitting both colors you are working with, one of them should not appear more dominant than the other. If you find that this is the case for you and both of your colors appear the same, you might not have to worry about dominance.

How to Work with Three Colors in a Round

When I work with three colors in one round, I keep the first color I'm using to the right of me and always pull it over the other two colors from the top position. I keep the second color I'm using in front of me (in the middle of the other two colors) and always pull it from that middle position (under the first color and over the third color). I keep the third color I'm using to the left of me and always pull it under the other two colors from the bottom position. Use whatever method works best for you! Just be careful to keep your yarn tidy as you knit so it doesn't get tangled.

How to Carry Floats and Catch Long Floats

Floats are the strands of yarn that are carried across the inside of your work. They are created when you switch colors as you knit, and you need to "carry" the yarn you aren't using behind the stitches of your working yarn to the next place it is used. My biggest tip is to never pull those floats too tightly, or your hat may appear puckered or narrow and will not have the stretch designed for it to fit properly. Keep it loose, my friends! I often give a gentle tug to my floats as I work to make sure they have enough slack.

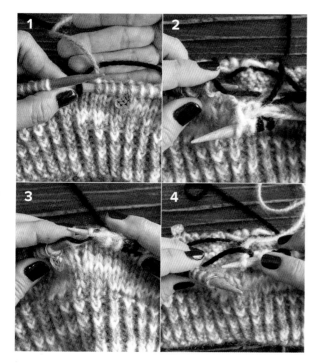

Typically, when you carry yarn behind fewer than six stitches, you don't have to worry about long floats or "catching" your floats. But, when you have a series of six or more stitches of one color, you will be carrying your unused color behind those stitches, and that will create a long float that you most likely will want to "catch" so it doesn't get snagged on anything when you wear your finished work. There are a variety of ways to catch long floats, and I will describe a super simple method for you! As always, use the technique that works best for you!

Easy catch method: Float the unused color, making sure to leave plenty of slack, in the round you are working.

Then, on the next round, when you reach the middle of the long float from the previous round, pick it up with your left needle and knit it together with the next stitch.

That's it! Done and done, my friends.

How to Carry Up Your Yarn

When you switch between colors as you knit a colorwork piece, one way to minimize the number of tails you have to weave in at the end is to "carry up" your yarn to the next round as you go instead of cutting it after each color change.

An easy way to do this is to wrap your working yarn counterclockwise once around the unused color you are carrying up at the beginning of a round when it comes to a color change. If you knit several rounds in your working yarn and don't use the other color, you don't need to repeat the wrapping process for every round, but rather every couple of rounds.

Just make sure to keep your yarn nice and tidy after you wrap it so it doesn't get tangled. This is especially important if you are working with two new colors and carrying up a third or fourth that isn't being used—keep the wrapped, unused yarn you are carrying up out of the way of your working yarn.

Long-Tail Cast-On Method

While there are plenty of methods for casting on, I used the long-tail cast-on method for all of the patterns in this book. If you choose to do the same, I recommend not casting on too tightly to avoid having a tight edge on your brim. And definitely feel free to use whatever cast-on method you are most comfortable with when making hats.

How to Block Your Finished Hat

Blocking is like magic when you're knitting colorwork, my friends, and I pretty much block all my finished items.

Like with most everything in knitting, there are different ways to block your finished pieces. Blocking is simply a method of getting your knits wet by submerging them in water or using a hand-held steamer with the end goal of smoothing out the stitches and setting the size. Some knitters refer to blocking as giving their knits a nice "bath" when they soak them in water with a gentle wool wash.

For lighter weight yarns, I waffle between wet blocking and steam blocking depending on the individual piece. For pieces that use heavier weight yarn, I tend to steam block because it takes less time to dry. In both cases, you get your knits wet using your preferred method and then lay them flat on a blocking mat to dry, pinning them into place if desired. There are mats you can buy specifically for blocking, but I just use a 2 x 2–foot (61 x 61–cm) foam square that is about 0.5 inch (1 cm) thick—nothing fancy. (I originally bought it to be used as flooring for my kids to play on when they were younger.) If you don't have this type of mat handy, you can pretty much use any flat surface that won't be damaged by dampness to lay out your knits as they dry.

BOLD
Beginnings

This is where it all starts, my friends. This is right where you want to be if you love to knit and you've never tried colorwork before. It's time for the artist within you to shine! Let the patterns in these pages become your canvas while your yarn and knitting needles serve as paint and brushes, helping you create some beautiful pieces.

This chapter is filled with bold yet beginner-friendly patterns designed to grab your attention and inspire you to really play with color combinations. Each pattern uses only two colors, introducing you to the concept of working with more than one strand of yarn at a time without it being overwhelming.

Zig Zaggity (page 33) allows you to explore a playful motif with repeats that become super rhythmic as you knit. You'll see a striking, horizontal chevron pattern begin to form in To the Left (page 41) after you work each round. Swirl Power (page 19) features a whimsical design to keep you engaged with every twist and turn all the way through the top of the crown.

Think of each of these patterns as an opportunity to create your own piece of art. You get to decide if you want to make something bright by choosing an adventurous color combination like hot pink and neon yellow, for example. Or maybe you prefer a more subtle approach, pairing a silvery gray with black? It's totally your choice!

So grab some skeins and listen to what colors speak to you. I truly believe that as long as you choose hues with high contrast, there really is no wrong combination when it comes to knitting colorwork. Each piece you create is unique, and that's what makes it so beautifully special. You're the artist, and you get to make your own masterpieces!

SWIRL POWER

I designed Swirl Power to be a hat full of whimsy and fun. This pattern is written for adult and child sizes, so you can even make a matching hat for your mini-me! Go with a fun hot pink and pale pink yarn pairing or go dramatic with black and white. Whatever color combo you choose, you will create a twisting visual effect as the design continues through the very top of the crown. I hope you have so much fun with every stitch!

Construction

This hat is worked in the round seamlessly from the brim to the crown.

Size

Measurements and information pertaining to child and adult sizes will be noted throughout this pattern as follows: Child (Adult). See the Finished Measurements section below.

This is a fitted hat, designed for the average Child (Adult) head measuring up to 19 (22)"/48 (55) cm. If you do not meet gauge in the stranded pattern (main body of the hat) with the suggested needles, change your needle size to meet gauge and ensure you achieve the right fit. Also, if you choose to use a single-ply yarn that does not stretch, you might consider increasing the circumference by casting on 42 (48) stitches instead of 36 (42) stitches. Any modification will affect the amount of yarn used.

Finished Measurements

Circumference: 15.25 (17.75)"/38 (44) cm

Height: 8 (9.25)"/20 (23) cm

If you use a single-ply yarn that does not stretch, or if you prefer a hat with added height, modifications can be found in the Modifications section. Any modification will affect the amount of yarn used.

Materials

Yarn

Approximately 69 (87) yds/64 (80) m total of super bulky yarn in two contrasting colors

Color A: 42 (53) yds/39 (49) m

Color B: 27 (34) yds/25 (32) m

Shown In

Malabrigo Yarn Rasta (100% Merino wool), 90 yds (82 m) per 5.3 oz (150 g)

Color A: Fucsia

Color B: Valentina

Recommended Yarn Substitution

Lion Brand® Yarn Wool-Ease® Thick & Quick® (80% acrylic, 20% wool), 106 yds (97 m) per 6 oz (170 g)

Suggested Needles

US 13 (9 mm) 16" (40 cm) circular knitting needles, or size needed to meet gauge

US 15 (10 mm) 16" (40 cm) circular knitting needles, or size needed to meet gauge

US 15 (10 mm) double-pointed needles or circular knitting needles with a longer cord for Magic Loop method (page 165), or size needed to meet gauge

Notions

Scissors

Stitch marker

Tapestry needle

Gauge

9 sts = 4" (10 cm) and 7 rnds = 2" (5 cm) in 1 x 1 ribbing (unstretched) using US 13 (9 mm) needles

9.5 sts x 12 rnds = 4" (10 cm) square in the stranded pattern (main body of the hat) using US 15 (10 mm) needles

Abbreviations

dpns = double-pointed needles

k = knit

k2tog = knit two together

p = purl

rnd(s) = round(s)

st(s) = stitch(es)

Tips to Help You Visualize Your Project and Get You Started

It's time to head to your local yarn shop or dive into your stash to pick out the yarn you'd like to use for **Color A** *and* **Color B**. **Color A** *will be used to cast on and it will form your brim. From there, both colors are pretty balanced throughout the rest of the hat.*

As a reminder, you can refer to the Colorwork Basics section (page 9) if you need help with any of the techniques used in this pattern.

I cannot stress enough the importance of keeping your floats loose, my friends, especially if you are using a single-ply super bulky yarn that does not stretch.

PATTERN

Brim

Using US 13 (9 mm) circular knitting needles, cast on 36 (42) sts using **Color A**. Place a stitch marker and join in the round.

Rnds 1–7 (**Color A**): *k1, p1; repeat from * to end, until brim measures 2.25" (6 cm) from cast-on.

Body

Please read through the following notes and possible modifications before beginning the chart.

Switch to US 15 (10 mm) circular knitting needles and follow the chart, working rounds 8–20 (8–23).

Each stitch shown in the chart is a knit stitch. Each section of 6 stitches is repeated 6 (7) times per round.

Modifications

Try on the hat after you complete the chart to determine whether you'd like to make modifications to the height.

Your hat should measure about 6.5 (7.5)"/16 (19) cm from the cast-on edge after you complete round 20 (round 23), resulting in an 8 (9.25)"/20 (23)-cm-tall hat after you finish the decrease instructions below.

Child: Work **Crown B**.

Adult: Work **Crown A**.

If your hat **does not** measure roughly 6.5 (7.5)"/16 (19) cm from the cast-on edge after you complete round 20 (round 23) or you prefer a hat with some slouch, you can repeat certain rounds as follows. Any modification will affect the amount of yarn used.

Child: Repeat rounds 9–11 once and then work **Crown A** or repeat rounds 9–14 once and work **Crown B**.

Adult: Repeat rounds 12–14 once and then work **Crown B** or repeat rounds 12–17 once and work **Crown A**.

Swirl Power Chart

Please note the **two different decrease sections** and follow the instructions that match your measurements or repeats for the child/adult hat you are working on.

Switch to dpns or Magic Loop method (page 165) when your stitches become too tight on your needles.

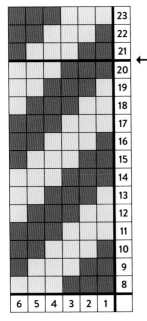

← Chart for child version ends after completing round 20.

Color A	
Color B	

Crown A

Rnd 24 (30): *k1 (**Color B**), k2tog (**Color B**), k1 (**Color A**), k2tog (**Color A**); repeat from * to end. [24 (28) sts]

Rnd 25 (31): *k2 (**Color B**), k2 (**Color A**); repeat from * to end.

Rnd 26 (32): *k2tog (**Color B**), k2tog (**Color A**); repeat from * to end. [12 (14) sts]

Rnd 27 (33): *k1 (**Color B**), k1 (**Color A**); repeat from * to end.

Crown B

Rnd 21 (27): *k1 (**Color A**), k2tog (**Color A**), k1 (**Color B**), k2tog (**Color B**); repeat from * to end. [24 (28) sts]

Rnd 22 (28): *k2 (**Color A**), k2 (**Color B**); repeat from * to end.

Rnd 23 (29): *k2tog (**Color A**), k2tog (**Color B**); repeat from * to end. [12 (14) sts]

Rnd 24 (30): *k1 (**Color A**), k1 (**Color B**); repeat from * to end.

Finishing

Cut **Color A** and **Color B**, making sure to leave tails about 12" (30 cm) long. Thread both tails through a tapestry needle and then weave them through the live stitches to take your work off your needles. Pull tails tightly to close the top of your hat.

Weave in all remaining ends.

Give your work a gentle horizontal tug to stretch out those floats and help shape your hat. I don't usually block my super bulky hats because they tend to take a long time to dry, and gentle stretching seems to do the trick just fine. If you would like to block this hat, however, I would suggest steam blocking.

STRIPES, STRIPES, BABY!

Starting with a fun, striped brim, this design features a playful mix of horizontal and vertical stripes that will grab your attention from the get-go. Knit with a worsted weight yarn and designed with a little bit of slouch, this hat is lightweight enough to make an awesome, everyday accessory for fall or spring. And with only two colors used throughout this pattern, you'll gain confidence and be able to boost your colorwork game with each stitch. Once you're done, this hat is sure to turn all the heads every time you wear it!

Construction

This hat is worked in the round seamlessly from the brim to the crown.

Size

One size. See the Finished Measurements section below.

This hat is designed with a bit of slouch for an adult head measuring up to 22" (55 cm). If you do not meet gauge in the stranded pattern (main body of the hat) with the suggested needles, change your needle size to meet gauge and ensure you achieve the right fit.

Finished Measurements

Circumference: 20.25" (51 cm)

Height: 9.75" (24 cm)

Materials

Yarn

Approximately 157 yds (144 m) total of worsted weight yarn in two contrasting colors

Color A: 85 yds (78 m)

Color B: 72 yds (66 m)

Shown In

OMG Yarn (Balls) Liberty (100% superwash Merino wool), 220 yds (202 m) per 3.5 oz (100 g)

Color A: Survivor

Color B: Dragon Breath

Recommended Yarn Substitution

Lion Brand Yarn Wool-Ease (80% acrylic, 20% wool), 197 yds (180 m) per 3 oz (85 g)

Suggested Needles

US 7 (4.5 mm) 16" (40 cm) circular knitting needles, or size needed to meet gauge

US 9 (5.5 mm) 16" (40 cm) circular knitting needles, or size needed to meet gauge

US 9 (5.5 mm) double-pointed needles or US 9 (5.5 mm) circular knitting needles with a longer cord for Magic Loop method (page 165), or size needed to meet gauge

Notions

Scissors

Stitch marker

Tapestry needle

Gauge

20 sts = 4" (10 cm) and 9 rnds = 1.5" (4 cm) in 1 x 1 ribbing (unstretched) using US 7 (4.5 mm) needles

16.5 sts x 20 rnds = 4" (10 cm) square in the stranded pattern (main body of the hat) using US 9 (5.5 mm) needles

Abbreviations

dpns = double-pointed needles

k = knit

k2tog = knit two together

p = purl

rnd(s) = round(s)

st(s) = stitch(es)

Tips to Help You Visualize Your Project and Get You Started

As much as this design entices me to celebrate every single bright color combo, I also love the idea of a neutral version in black and taupe. The colors are balanced throughout, so just pick a yarn pairing that speaks to you right now. You can always make another if your mood changes, right?

As a reminder, you can refer to the Colorwork Basics section (page 9) if you need help with any of the techniques used in this pattern.

PATTERN

Brim

Using US 7 (4.5 mm) circular knitting needles, cast on 84 sts using **Color A**. Place a stitch marker and join in the round.

Rnd 1 (**Color A**): *k1, p1; repeat from * to end.

Rnds 2–3 (**Color B**): *k1, p1; repeat from * to end.

Rnds 4–5 (**Color A**): *k1, p1; repeat from * to end.

Rnds 6–7 (**Color B**): *k1, p1; repeat from * to end.

Rnds 8–9 (**Color A**): *k1, p1; repeat from * to end.

Body

Please read through all of the following notes before beginning the chart.

Switch to US 9 (5.5 mm) circular knitting needles and follow the chart, working rounds 10-43.

All stitches shown in the chart are knit stitches. Each section of 4 stitches is repeated 21 times per round.

As you knit the hat, there will be a few spots where you will want to carry up your yarn when it is not being used. At the beginning of rounds 20, 27 and 40, you will want to carry up **Color A**. You can do this by wrapping **Color B** (your working yarn) counterclockwise once around **Color A** (your unused yarn) and then continuing to work the chart. At the beginning of rounds 24 and 36, you will want to carry up **Color B**. You can do this by wrapping **Color A** (your working yarn) counterclockwise once around **Color B** (your unused yarn) and then continuing to work the chart. I will indicate these spots on the chart as a friendly reminder!

You also will want to minimize the appearance of jogs in your stripes in a few places. Jogs occur when you're knitting in the round because you're essentially knitting in a spiral. So each round starts stacking on top of the next, and that can sometimes result in a jagged look at the join. To minimize the appearance of jogs in this pattern, you can simply slip the first stitch of the second round knit in your new color. This is also indicated on the chart. For more on jogs, see the Techniques section (page 164).

Cut **Color B** after round 40.

Stripes, Stripes, Baby! Chart

Your hat should measure about 8.25" (21 cm) from the cast-on edge after completing the chart. If it does not, or if you prefer more slouch, you can continue knitting in the round using **Color A** until you reach that measurement/your desired height before moving on to the **Crown** section. Any modification will affect the amount of yarn used.

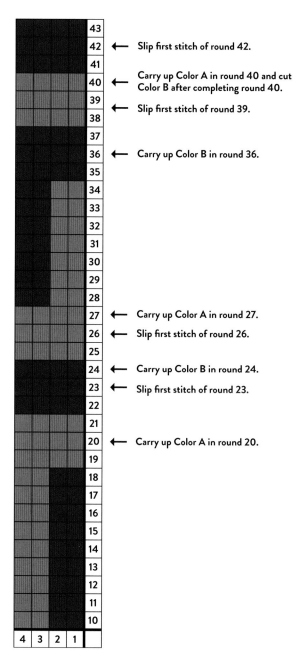

| | Color A | ■ |
| | Color B | ▨ |

Slip first stitch of round 42.

Carry up Color A in round 40 and cut Color B after completing round 40.

Slip first stitch of round 39.

Carry up Color B in round 36.

Carry up Color A in round 27.

Slip first stitch of round 26.

Carry up Color B in round 24.

Slip first stitch of round 23.

Carry up Color A in round 20.

Crown

Switch to dpns or Magic Loop method (page 165) when your stitches become too tight on your needles.

Use **Color A** for all remaining rounds.

Rnd 44: *k4, k2tog; repeat from * to end. [70 sts]

Rnd 45: k to end.

Rnd 46: *k3, k2tog; repeat from * to end. [56 sts]

Rnd 47: k to end.

Rnd 48: *k2, k2tog; repeat from * to end. [42 sts]

Rnd 49: k to end.

Rnd 50: *k1, k2tog; repeat from * to end. [28 sts]

Rnd 51: k to end.

Rnd 52: *k2tog; repeat from * to end. [14 sts]

Finishing

Cut **Color A**, making sure to leave a tail about 12" (30 cm) long. Thread the tail through a tapestry needle and then weave it through the live stitches to take your work off your needles. Pull the tail tightly to close the top of your hat.

Weave in all remaining ends.

I recommend steam blocking this hat to smooth out your floats, shape it and help minimize the appearance of jogs in your stripes (see page 164 for more on jogs).

SERPENTINE

There are so many fun twists and turns all the way up through the crown with this pattern! I designed this hat with a textured, garter stitch brim packed with horizontal squiggles to play off of the vertical wiggles in the body of the hat. But if you prefer a traditional ribbed brim, I have you covered with instructions for that as well. No matter which brim option you choose, I hope you have the best time knitting this!

Construction

This hat is worked in the round seamlessly from the brim to the crown.

Size

One size. See the Finished Measurements section below.

This is a fitted hat designed for an adult head measuring up to 23" (58 cm). If you do not meet gauge in the stranded pattern (main body of the hat) with the suggested needles, change your needle size to meet gauge and ensure you achieve the right fit. The sizing can be adjusted by reducing or adding cast-on stitches in multiples of 6. Any modification will affect the amount of yarn used.

Finished Measurements

Circumference: 18.5" (46 cm)

Height: 9" (23 cm)

Gauge

12 sts = 4" (10 cm) and 14 rnds = 2.25" (6 cm) in garter stitch using US 9 (5.5 mm) needles

14.5 sts = 4" (10 cm) and 8 rnds = 2.25" (6 cm) in 1 x 1 ribbing (unstretched) using US 9 (5.5 mm) needles

13 sts x 16 rnds = 4" (10 cm) square in the stranded pattern (main body of the hat) using US 10.5 (6.5 mm) needles

Materials

Yarn

Approximately 107 yds (98 m) total of bulky weight yarn in two contrasting colors

Color A: 69 yds (64 m)

Color B: 38 yds (35 m)

Shown In

OMG Yarn (Balls) Yosemite (100% superwash Merino wool), 120 yds (110 m) per 3.5 oz (100 g)

Color A: Romulan Ale

Color B: Dragon Breath

Recommended Yarn Substitutions

Lion Brand Yarn Hue + Me (80% acrylic, 20% wool), 137 yds (125 m) per 4.4 oz (125 g)

Malabrigo Yarn Chunky (100% Merino wool), 104 yds (95 m) per 3.5 oz (100 g)

Suggested Needles

US 9 (5.5 mm) 16" (40 cm) circular knitting needles, or size needed to meet gauge

US 10.5 (6.5 mm) 16" (40 cm) circular knitting needles, or size needed to meet gauge

US 10.5 (6.5 mm) double-pointed needles or US 10.5 (6.5 mm) circular knitting needles with a longer cord for Magic Loop method (page 165), or size needed to meet gauge

Notions

Scissors

Stitch marker

Tapestry needle

Yarn pom or faux fur pom (optional)

Abbreviations

dpns = double-pointed needles

k = knit

p = purl

rnd(s) = round(s)

ssk = slip, slip, knit (slip two stitches knit-wise, one at a time, from the left needle onto the right needle; slip both stitches back to the left needle and knit them together through the back loop)

st(s) = stitch(es)

Tips to Help You Visualize Your Project and Get You Started

The hardest part about this one, my friends, is deciding if you want to go bold or go neutral. The detail of the garter stitch brim might show up best with lighter colors or bright colors, so that could be a consideration for you. And remember, there is also an option to knit a ribbed brim if you prefer that. If you choose the garter stitch brim, it will seem wider to you as you knit than a ribbed brim, and that is totally okay, as it stretches differently than ribbing.

Other than that, it's time to dive into your stash and start playing with color!

As a reminder, you can refer to the Colorwork Basics section (page 9) if you need help with any of the techniques used in this pattern.

PATTERN

Brim

Please note there are instructions for two brim options—pick your favorite! The garter stitch brim knits up wider and has a less snug fit than the 1 x 1 ribbed brim.

Using US 9 (5.5 mm) circular knitting needles, cast on 60 sts using **Color A**. Place a stitch marker and join in the round.

Option 1 (as shown): Garter Stitch Brim

Rnd 1: *p1; repeat from * to end.

Rnd 2: *k1; repeat from * to end.

Repeat rounds 1 and 2 six more times (seven times total) to create a 2.25" (6-cm) brim.

Option 2: 1 x 1 Ribbed Brim

Rnds 1–8: *k1, p1; repeat from * to end.

Body

Please read through the following notes before beginning the chart.

Switch to US 10.5 (6.5 mm) circular knitting needles and follow the chart on page 31, working rounds 1–20.

Each stitch shown in the chart is a knit stitch. Each section of 6 stitches is repeated 10 times per round.

Your hat should measure 7.25" (18 cm) after you complete the chart.

Serpentine Chart

						20
						19
						18
						17
						16
						15
						14
						13
						12
						11
						10
						9
						8
						7
						6
						5
						4
						3
						2
						1
6	5	4	3	2	1	

Color A	
Color B	

Crown

Switch to dpns or Magic Loop method (page 165) when your stitches become too tight on your needles.

You will alternate between **Color A** and **Color B** to complete the crown. Pay careful attention to the color designated for each set of stitches in each round.

Rnd 1: k1 (**Color A**), *ssk (**Color B**), k4 (**Color A**); repeat from * to last 5 sts then ssk (**Color B**), k3 (**Color A**). [50 sts]

Rnd 2: k1 (**Color A**), *k1 (**Color B**), ssk (**Color A**), k2 (**Color A**); repeat from * to last 4 sts then k1 (**Color B**), ssk (**Color A**), k1 (**Color A**). [40 sts]

Rnd 3: k1 (**Color A**), *k1 (**Color B**), k1 (**Color A**), ssk (**Color A**); repeat from * to last 3 sts then k1 (**Color B**), k1 (**Color A**) and slip last **Color A** st remaining on your left needle knit-wise onto your right needle. Remove stitch marker. Now, slip the first **Color A** st on your left needle knit-wise onto your right needle and knit the two slipped **Color A** sts together through the back loops. Replace marker. [30 sts]

Rnd 4: *k1 (**Color B**), ssk (**Color A**); repeat from * to end. [20 sts]

Rnd 5: *k1 (**Color B**), k1 (**Color A**); repeat from * to end. Cut **Color A**.

Rnd 6: *ssk (**Color B**); repeat from * to end. [10 sts]

Finishing

Cut **Color B**, making sure to leave a tail roughly 12" (30 cm) long. Thread the tail through a tapestry needle and then weave it through the live stitches to take your work off your needles. Pull the tail tightly to close the top of your hat. You may need to use a tapestry needle to pull **Color B** stitches over any **Color A** stitches that may peek through on your final decrease round.

Weave in all remaining ends.

Give your work a gentle horizontal tug to stretch out those floats and help shape your hat. I highly recommend steam blocking this hat to smooth out all your stitches.

ZIG ZAGGITY

Zigzags get me every time, my friends! They're super simple, and they have such a cool, bold look. Plus, once you get into knitting them, they become very rhythmic. This pattern features zigzags of varying widths and a fun crown that carries the colorwork through the top to create a floral design.

Construction

This hat is worked in the round seamlessly from the brim to the crown.

Size

One size. See the Finished Measurements section below.

This is a fitted hat designed for an adult head measuring up to 21" (53 cm). If you do not meet gauge in the stranded pattern (main body of the hat) with the suggested needles, change your needle size to meet gauge and ensure you achieve the right fit.

Finished Measurements

Circumference: 17.25" (43 cm)

Height: 8.5" (21 cm)

Gauge

17 sts = 4" (10 cm) and 7 rnds = 1.5" (4 cm) in 1 x 1 ribbing (unstretched) using US 9 (5.5 mm) needles

14 sts x 17 rnds = 4" (10 cm) square in the stranded pattern (main body of the hat) using US 11 (8 mm) needles

Materials

Yarn

Approximately 102 yds (94 m) total of bulky weight yarn in two contrasting colors

Color A: 57 yds (53 m)

Color B: 45 yds (42 m)

Shown In

Neighborhood Fiber Co. Organic Studio Chunky (100% organic Merino wool), 125 yds (115 m) per 4 oz (114 g)

Color A: Logan Circle

Color B: Lake Evesham

Recommended Yarn Substitutions

Malabrigo Yarn Chunky (100% Merino wool), 104 yds (95 m) per 3.5 oz (100 g)

Lion Brand Yarn Hue + Me (80% acrylic, 20% wool), 137 yds (125 m) per 4.4 oz (125 g)

Suggested Needles

US 9 (5.5 mm) 16" (40 cm) circular knitting needles, or size needed to meet gauge

US 11 (8 mm) 16" (40 cm) circular knitting needles, or size needed to meet gauge

US 11 (8 mm) double-pointed needles or US 11 (8 mm) circular knitting needles with a longer cord for Magic Loop method (page 165), or size needed to meet gauge

Notions

Scissors

Stitch marker

Tapestry needle

Abbreviations

dpns = double-pointed needles

k = knit

k2tog = knit two together

k3tog = knit three together

p = purl

rnd(s) = round(s)

ssk = slip, slip, knit (slip two stitches knit-wise, one at a time, from the left needle onto the right needle; slip both stitches back to the left needle and knit them together through the back loop)

st(s) = stitch(es)

Tips to Help You Visualize Your Project and Get You Started

The balance of color throughout this hat is pretty even, so you can just pick two colors that speak to you without worrying about one being more dominant than the other.

As a reminder, you can refer to the Colorwork Basics section (page 9) if you need help with any of the techniques used in this pattern.

PATTERN

Brim

Using US 9 (5.5 mm) circular knitting needles, cast on 60 sts using **Color A**. Place a stitch marker and join in the round.

Rnds 1–7 (**Color A**): *k1, p1; repeat from * to end.

Body

Please read through all of the following notes before beginning the chart.

Switch to US 11 (8 mm) circular knitting needles and follow the chart, working rounds 8–30.

Each stitch shown in the chart is a knit stitch. Each section of 6 stitches is repeated 10 times per round.

If you would like to minimize the appearance of jogs in your zigzags, begin with a new strand of yarn for each color change (rounds 11, 14, 19, 22, 25 and 28; see page 164 for more on jogs). These spots will be indicated on the chart as a friendly reminder if you choose this method. Do not weave in your ends until you complete your hat. There is an easy trick to help erase those jogs in the Techniques section (page 164) at the end of this book!

If you aren't bothered by the jogs or if you prefer fewer tails to weave in, you can carry up your yarn instead.

Zig Zaggity Chart

Your hat should measure roughly 7" (18 cm) once you complete the chart, resulting in an 8.5" (21-cm) hat after you complete the **Crown** section. If you prefer a taller hat, you can repeat rounds 25–30 once more, which will add roughly 1.5" (4 cm) to the height, before moving on to the **Crown** section. Any modification will affect the amount of yarn used.

Do not cut **Color A** or **Color B** after completing the chart as both colors will be used in the **Crown** section.

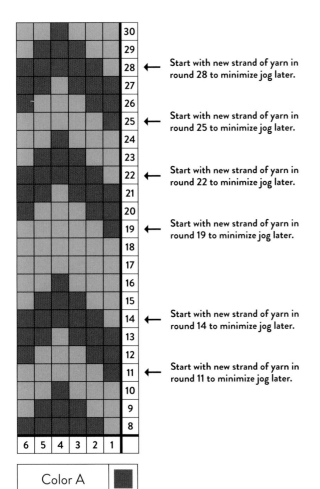

Start with new strand of yarn in round 28 to minimize jog later.

Start with new strand of yarn in round 25 to minimize jog later.

Start with new strand of yarn in round 22 to minimize jog later.

Start with new strand of yarn in round 19 to minimize jog later.

Start with new strand of yarn in round 14 to minimize jog later.

Start with new strand of yarn in round 11 to minimize jog later.

| Color A | ■ |
| Color B | ■ |

Crown

Switch to dpns or Magic Loop method (page 165) when your stitches become too tight on your needles.

You will alternate between **Color A** and **Color B** to complete the crown. Pay careful attention to the color designated for each set of stitches in each round.

Rnd 31: *k1 (**Color B**), ssk (**Color B**), k1 (**Color A**), k2tog (**Color B**); repeat from * to end. [40 sts]

Rnd 32: *k2 (**Color B**), k1 (**Color A**), k1 (**Color B**); repeat from * to end.

Rnd 33: k2 (**Color B**), *k1 (**Color A**), k3tog (**Color B**); repeat from * until last 2 sts, then k1 (**Color A**). Now, slip the last st on your left needle purl-wise onto your right needle. Remove the marker. Then, slip the first st on your right needle (the st you just moved) back onto your left needle and k3tog (**Color B**). Replace the marker. [20 sts]

Rnd 34: *k1 (**Color A**), k1 (**Color B**); repeat from * to end. Cut **Color B**, leaving a tail to weave in later.

Rnd 35: *k2tog (**Color A**); repeat from * to end. [10 sts]

Finishing

Cut **Color A**, making sure to leave a tail roughly 12" (30 cm) long. Thread the tail through a tapestry needle and then weave it through the live stitches to take your work off your needles. Pull the tail tightly to close the top of your hat.

Weave in all remaining ends.

Give your work a gentle horizontal tug to stretch out those floats and help shape your hat. I steam blocked mine—feel free to do the same!

FLIP SIDE

In Flip Side, the design begins to form in the opposite color combo as you work this hat from the bottom up. There are just color combos galore with this baby! And since it uses super bulky yarn, it knits up super quickly as well. As a bonus, this is a very beginner-friendly pattern for those new to colorwork, and it would make a great gift for everyone on your list because it's so fast to make. But I totally understand if you can't resist keeping one of these cozy beauties for yourself. Your secret is safe with me!

Construction

This hat is worked in the round seamlessly from the brim to the crown.

Size

One size. See the Finished Measurements section below.

This is a fitted hat designed for an adult head measuring up to 22" (55 cm). If you do not meet gauge in the stranded pattern (main body of the hat) with the suggested needles, change your needle size to meet gauge and ensure you achieve the right fit.

Finished Measurements

Circumference: 19.75" (49 cm)

Height: 9" (23 cm)

Materials

Yarn

Approximately 73 yds (67 m) total of super bulky weight yarn in two contrasting colors

Color A: 43 yds (40 m)

Color B: 30 yds (28 m)

Shown In

Mountain Laurel Fiber Co. The Squish (100% superwash Merino wool), 126 yds (116 m) per 9 oz (255 g)

Color A: Plum-Berry

Color B: Sap

Recommended Yarn Substitution

Lion Brand Yarn Wool-Ease Thick & Quick (80% acrylic, 20% wool), 106 yds (97 m) per 6 oz (170 g)

Suggested Needles

US 13 (9 mm) 16" (40 cm) circular knitting needles, or size needed to meet gauge

US 15 (10 mm) 16" (40 cm) circular knitting needles, or size needed to meet gauge

US 15 (10 mm) double-pointed needles or US 15 (10 mm) circular knitting needles with a longer cord for Magic Loop method (page 165), or size needed to meet gauge

Notions

Scissors

Stitch marker

Tapestry needle

Gauge

9 sts = 4" (10 cm) and 6 rnds = 1.75" (4 cm) in 1 x 1 ribbing (unstretched) using US 13 (9 mm) needles

8.5 sts x 11 rnds = 4" (10 cm) square in the stranded pattern (main body of the hat) using US 15 (10 mm) needles

Abbreviations

dpns = double-pointed needles

k = knit

k2tog = knit two together

p = purl

rnd(s) = round(s)

ssk = slip, slip, knit (slip two stitches knit-wise, one at a time, from the left needle onto the right needle; slip both stitches back to the left needle and knit them together through the back loop)

st(s) = stitch(es)

Tips to Help You Visualize Your Project and Get You Started

This hat features a bold design with a pretty even balance of colors throughout, so the sky's the limit with yarn pairings. Pick a charcoal gray and cream for a neutral vibe or go for a color explosion with lime green and orange. It's totally up to you!

As a reminder, you can refer to the Colorwork Basics section (page 9) if you need help with any of the techniques used in this pattern.

I cannot stress enough the importance of keeping your floats loose, my friends, especially if you are using a single-ply super bulky yarn that does not stretch.

PATTERN

Brim

Using US 13 (9 mm) circular knitting needles, cast on 42 sts using **Color A**. Place a stitch marker and join in the round.

Rnds 1–6 (**Color A**): *k1, p1; repeat from * to end.

Body

Please read through the following notes before beginning the chart.

Switch to US 15 (10 mm) circular knitting needles and follow the chart on page 39, working rounds 7–22.

Each stitch shown on the chart is a knit stitch. Each section of 6 stitches is repeated 7 times per round.

Cut **Color A** after round 21.

Flip Side Chart

Your hat should measure about 7.5" (19 cm) from the cast-on edge after you complete the chart, resulting in a 9" (23-cm)-tall hat after you finish the **Crown** instructions.

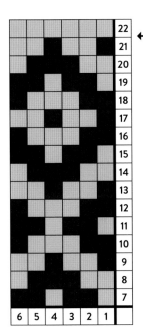

→ **Cut Color A after completing round 21.**

6	5	4	3	2	1	

Color A	■
Color B	▨

Crown

Switch to dpns or Magic Loop method (page 165) when your stitches become too tight on your needles.

Use **Color B** for all remaining rounds.

Rnd 23: k1, k2tog, *k1, ssk, k1, k2tog; repeat from * to last 3 sts, then k1, ssk. [28 sts]

Rnd 24: k to end.

Rnd 25: *k2tog; repeat from * to end. [14 sts]

Rnd 26: k to end.

Finishing

Cut **Color B**, making sure to leave a tail about 12" (30 cm) long. Thread the tail through a tapestry needle and then weave it through the live stitches to take your work off your needles. Pull the tail tightly to close the top of your hat.

Weave in all remaining ends.

Give your work a gentle horizontal tug to stretch out those floats and help shape your hat. I don't usually block my super bulky hats because they tend to take a long time to dry, and gentle stretching seems to do the trick just fine. If you would like to block this hat, however, I would suggest steam blocking.

TO THE LEFT

To the Left features a bold, horizontal chevron pattern that leaves so many possibilities for you to experiment with color! This pattern is very beginner friendly for those new to colorwork. You'll only knit with two colors, find short floats and create a simple crown that could totally be topped off by a colorful yarn or faux fur pom. And since it's made with super bulky yarn, it's also a quick knit! This is one of those patterns you may find yourself returning to again and again for last-minute gifts, to match a certain outfit or even whip up in your favorite team colors!

Construction

This hat is worked in the round seamlessly from the brim to the crown.

Size

One size. See the Finished Measurements section below.

This hat is designed for an adult head measuring up to 22" (55 cm). If you do not meet gauge in the stranded pattern (main body of the hat) with the suggested needles, change your needle size to meet gauge and ensure you achieve the right fit. The sizing also can be adjusted by reducing or adding cast-on stitches in multiples of 6. Any modification will affect the amount of yarn used.

Finished Measurements

Circumference: 18.75" (47 cm)

Height: 9.5" (24 cm)

Gauge

9 sts = 4" (10 cm) and 7 rnds = 2" (5 cm) in 1 x 1 ribbing (unstretched) using US 13 (9 mm) needles

9 sts x 12 rnds = 4" (10 cm) square in the stranded pattern (main body of the hat) using US 15 (10 mm) needles

Materials

Yarn

Approximately 79 yds (73 m) total of super bulky weight yarn in two contrasting colors

Color A: 54 yds (50 m)

Color B: 25 yds (23 m)

Shown In

Lion Brand Yarn Wool-Ease Thick & Quick (80% acrylic, 20% wool), 106 yds (97 m) per 6 oz (170 g)

Color A: Black

Color B: Cranberry, Pumpkin, Mustard, Grass, Denim or Iris

Suggested Needles

US 13 (9 mm) 16" (40 cm) circular knitting needles, or size needed to meet gauge

US 15 (10 mm) 16" (40 cm) circular knitting needles, or size needed to meet gauge

US 15 (10 mm) double-pointed needles or US 15 (10 mm) circular knitting needles with a longer cord for Magic Loop method (page 165), or size needed to meet gauge

Notions

Scissors

Stitch marker

Tapestry needle

Abbreviations

dpns = double-pointed needles

k = knit

k2tog = knit two together

p = purl

rnd(s) = round(s)

st(s) = stitch(es)

Tips to Help You Visualize Your Project and Get You Started

*This design gives you an awesome chance to play with color. You'll use **Color A** to cast on, create the brim and finish the crown, so you might want to start by picking that color. In the main body of the hat, **Color A** and **Color B** are pretty evenly balanced.*

As a reminder, you can refer to the Colorwork Basics section (page 9) if you need help with any of the techniques used in this pattern.

I cannot stress the importance of loose floats enough, especially if you are using a single-ply super bulky yarn that does not stretch.

PATTERN

Brim

Using US 13 (9 mm) circular knitting needles, cast on 42 sts using **Color A**. Place a stitch marker and join in the round.

Rnds 1–7 (**Color A**): *k1, p1; repeat from * to end.

Body

Please read through the following notes before beginning the chart.

Switch to US 15 (10 mm) circular knitting needles and follow the chart, working rounds 8–24.

Each stitch shown in the chart is a knit stitch. Each section of 6 stitches is repeated 7 times per round.

Cut **Color B** once you complete round 22.

To the Left Chart

Your hat should measure about 8" (20 cm) from the cast-on edge once you complete the chart, resulting in a 9.5" (24-cm)-tall hat after you finish the **Crown** section. If your hat does not measure roughly 8" (20 cm) from the cast-on edge once you complete the chart or if you prefer a hat with more slouch, you can continue knitting in the round using **Color A** until it reaches that measurement/your desired height. Any modification will affect the amount of yarn used.

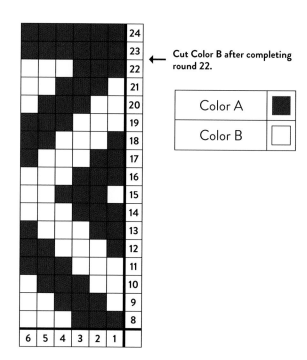

Cut Color B after completing round 22.

	Color A	■
	Color B	□

Crown

Use **Color A** for all remaining rounds.

Switch to dpns or Magic Loop method (page 165) when your stitches become too tight on your needles.

Rnd 25: *k4, k2tog; repeat from * to end. [35 sts]

Rnd 26: k to end.

Rnd 27: *k3, k2tog; repeat from * to end. [28 sts]

Rnd 28: k to end.

Rnd 29: *k2tog; repeat from * to end. [14 sts]

Finishing

Cut **Color A**, making sure to leave a tail about 12" (30 cm) long. Thread the tail through a tapestry needle and then weave it through the live stitches to take your work off your needles. Pull the tail tightly to close the top of your hat.

Weave in all remaining ends.

Give your work a gentle horizontal tug to stretch out those floats and help shape your hat. I don't usually block my super bulky hats because they tend to take a long time to dry, and gentle stretching seems to do the trick just fine. If you would like to block this hat, however, I would suggest steam blocking.

TAKING
Shape

This is where you take the next step on your colorwork journey, my friends! In this chapter, you will find patterns with simple shapes that form playful, eye-catching designs. The patterns in these pages encourage you to build on basic colorwork skills and expand your exploration of color combinations.

In Heartstrings (page 47) and Whirligig (page 55), you'll get a chance to experiment with combining three colors in each pattern, although you'll only ever work with two colors at any one time. Wish upon a star with Twinkle (page 59), which makes for a perfect mommy-and-me project, as it's written for adult and child sizes. And Hopscotch (page 71) is a whimsical pattern that includes a super easy trick for catching long floats—don't worry, it's not as scary as it sounds. I promise!

All of the patterns included in this chapter are designed to slowly incorporate new tricks and skills into your colorwork knitting in a way that grows your confidence and doesn't overwhelm you with too much at once.

This is such an exciting stage for you, my friends! Let the yarn and the colors be your guide. Use the new skills and confidence you'll gain in this chapter to advance your colorwork game. Step out of your comfort zone and let yourself explore the possibility of new color pairings. Be the artist you were born to be! Remember, each piece you create is its own little masterpiece, and it's beautiful because you made it.

HEART-STRINGS

Little strings of hearts dance across the body of this design to create a sense of whimsy and magic. I used only three colors for this pattern, but you could totally knit up a scrappy version with a black background, for example, and then use two different colors for each of the heartstrings! This is a design that will keep enticing you to knit it again to see what color combo you'll come up with next.

Construction

This hat is worked in the round seamlessly from the brim to the crown.

Size

One size. See the Finished Measurements section on the next page.

This hat is designed with just a little bit of slouch for an adult head measuring up to 22" (55 cm). If you do not meet gauge in the stranded pattern (main body of the hat) with the suggested needles, change your needle size to meet gauge and ensure you achieve the right fit.

Materials

Yarn

Approximately 162 yds (149 m) total of worsted weight yarn in three contrasting colors

Color A: 53 yds (49 m)

Color B: 36 yds (33 m)

Color C: 73 yds (67 m)

Shown In

Mitchell's Creations Bayou (100% superwash Merino wool), 218 yds (199 m) per 3.5 oz (100 g)

Color A: Bordeaux

Color B: Sweetest Hangover

Color C: Boyfriend Jeans

Recommended Yarn Substitutions

Malabrigo Yarn Rios (100% superwash Merino wool), 210 yds (192 m) per 3.5 oz (100 g)

Lion Brand Yarn Wool-Ease (80% acrylic, 20% wool), 197 yds (180 m) per 3 oz (85 g)

Suggested Needles

US 6 (4 mm) 16" (40 cm) circular knitting needles, or size needed to meet gauge

US 8 (5 mm) 16" (40 cm) circular knitting needles, or size needed to meet gauge

US 8 (5 mm) double-pointed needles or US 8 (5 mm) circular knitting needles with a longer cord for Magic Loop method (page 165), or size needed to meet gauge

Notions

Scissors

Stitch marker

Tapestry needle

Finished Measurements

Circumference: 19" (48 cm)

Height: 9" (23 cm)

Gauge

23 sts = 4" (10 cm) and 9 rnds = 1.25" (3 cm) in 1 x 1 ribbing (unstretched) using US 6 (4 mm) needles

19 sts x 27 rnds = 4" (10 cm) square in the stranded pattern (main body of the hat) using US 8 (5 mm) needles

Abbreviations

dpns = double-pointed needles

k = knit

k2tog = knit two together

p = purl

rnd(s) = round(s)

st(s) = stitch(es)

Tips to Help You Visualize Your Project and Get You Started

*As you decide on colors for this hat, I recommend picking your background color (**Color C**) first to make it easier to figure out how well the heartstrings will pop against it. You can totally go with the heart theme of the design and choose pinks, reds or purples. Or you can use unexpected colors like neon yellow, black and tan to give the pattern a completely different vibe. There's always that scrappy possibility, too, of choosing a neutral background and changing yarn pairings for each heartstring.*

As a reminder, you can refer to the Colorwork Basics section (page 9) if you need help with any of the techniques used in this pattern.

PATTERN

Brim

Using US 6 (4 mm) circular knitting needles, cast on 90 sts using **Color A**. Place a stitch marker and join in the round.

Rnds 1–9 (**Color A**): *k1, p1; repeat from * to end.

Rnd 10 (**Color A**): *k1; repeat from * to end.

Body

Please read through all of the following notes before beginning the chart.

Switch to US 8 (5 mm) circular knitting needles and follow the chart, working rounds 11–25.

All stitches shown in the chart are knit stitches. Each section of 5 stitches is repeated 18 times per round.

You can choose to cut your yarn as you switch between colors or carry it up. For the sample I made, I carried up my yarn as I switched between colors to minimize the number of tails I had to weave in at the end. You can carry up your yarn by wrapping your working yarn counterclockwise once around your unused yarn and then continuing to work the chart. If you choose to do the same, just make sure to keep your yarn tidy as you begin each round so that colors do not get tangled. I will indicate the spots where I carried up my yarn on the chart to help you out.

There is one spot in the pattern where you will want to minimize the appearance of a jog in the **Color B** stripe toward the bottom of your hat. This can be done simply by slipping the first stitch of round 12 purl-wise and then continuing to knit the rest of the round according to the chart. I will indicate this spot next to the chart as a friendly reminder.

Heartstrings Chart

Your hat should measure about 7.25" (18 cm) from the cast-on edge after completing the chart repetitions. If it does not, or if you prefer more slouch, you can continue to repeat round 51 in the **Crown** section until you reach that measurement/ your desired height before moving on to round 52. Any modification will affect the amount of yarn used. Cut **Color A** and **Color B**.

Color A	■
Color B	■
Color C	■

						25
						24	← Carry up Color A in round 24.
						23	← Carry up Color C in round 23.
						22
						21	← Carry up Color A in round 21.
						20	← Carry up Color B in round 20.
						19
						18	← Carry up Color B in round 18.
						17	← Carry up Color C in round 17.
						16
						15	← Carry up Color B in round 15.
						14
						13	← Carry up Color A in round 13.
						12	← Slip first stitch of round 12.
						11
5	4	3	2	1		

Work rounds 11–25 once.

Rounds 26–49: repeat Rounds 14–25 twice more before moving on to the Crown section.

Crown

Use **Color C** for all remaining rounds.

Switch to dpns or Magic Loop method (page 165) when your stitches become too tight on your needles.

Rnds 50–51: k to end.

Rnd 52: *k4, k2tog; repeat from * to end. [75 sts]

Rnd 53: k to end.

Rnd 54: *k3, k2tog; repeat from * to end. [60 sts]

Rnd 55: k to end.

Rnd 56: *k2, k2tog; repeat from * to end. [45 sts]

Rnd 57: k to end.

Rnd 58: *k1, k2tog; repeat from * to end. [30 sts]

Rnd 59: k to end.

Rnd 60: *k2tog; repeat from * to end. [15 sts]

Finishing

Cut **Color C**, making sure to leave a tail about 12" (30 cm) long. Thread the tail through a tapestry needle and then weave it through the live stitches to take your work off your needles. Pull the tail tightly to close the top of your hat.

Weave in all remaining ends.

I highly recommend blocking this hat to smooth out your floats, shape it and help minimize the appearance of jogs at the join by pinning them into place (see page 164 for more on jogs).

FLASH DASH

Those diagonal dashes knit up so quickly, my friends, that you'll have this baby done and on your head in a flash! You'll add the twisted rib stitch to your skillset with this design by knitting through the back loop on the brim. From there, this pattern will keep you engaged with each round as you start to see the pattern emerge. And with two colors throughout the crown to continue the design, the fun doesn't stop until you're finished!

Construction

This hat is worked in the round seamlessly from the brim to the crown.

Size

One size. See the Finished Measurements section below.

This is a fitted hat designed for an adult head measuring up to 22" (55 cm). If you do not meet gauge in the stranded pattern (main body of the hat) with the suggested needles, change your needle size to meet gauge and ensure you achieve the right fit.

Finished Measurements

Circumference: 19.75" (49 cm)

Height: 9" (23 cm)

Gauge

14 sts = 4" (10 cm) and 7 rnds = 1.5" (4 cm) in 1 x 1 twisted ribbing (unstretched) using US 9 (5.5 mm) needles

13 sts x 14 rnds = 4" (10 cm) square in the stranded pattern (main body of the hat) using US 11 (8 mm) needles

Materials

Yarn

Approximately 121 yds (111 m) total of bulky weight yarn in two contrasting colors

Color A: 63 yds (58 m)

Color B: 58 yds (54 m)

Shown In

Malabrigo Yarn Chunky (100% Merino wool), 104 yds (95 m) per 3.5 oz (100 g)

Color A: Sunset

Color B: Pollen

Recommended Yarn Substitution

Lion Brand Yarn Hue + Me (80% acrylic, 20% wool), 137 yds (125 m) per 4.4 oz (125 g)

Suggested Needles

US 9 (5.5 mm) 16" (40 cm) circular knitting needles, or size needed to meet gauge

US 11 (8 mm) 16" (40 cm) circular knitting needles, or size needed to meet gauge

US 11 (8 mm) double-pointed needles or US 11 (8 mm) circular knitting needles with a longer cord for Magic Loop method (page 165), or size needed to meet gauge

Notions

Scissors

Stitch marker

Tapestry needle

Abbreviations

dpns = double-pointed needles

k = knit

k1tbl = knit one stitch through the back loop

k2tog = knit two together

p = purl

rnd(s) = round(s)

st(s) = stitch(es)

Tips to Help You Visualize Your Project and Get You Started

*This is such a fun and fast knit for which you might spend more time picking out your colors than knitting the hat! There is a pretty even balance of colors in this hat, so I'd recommend just starting out with choosing your **Color A**, which you'll use to cast on and create the brim.*

As a reminder, you can refer to the Colorwork Basics section (page 9) if you need help with any of the techniques used in this pattern.

PATTERN

Brim

Using US 9 (5.5 mm) circular knitting needles, cast on 64 sts using **Color A**. Place a stitch marker and join in the round.

Rnds 1–7 (**Color A**): *k1tbl, p1; repeat from * to end.

Body

Please read through the following notes before beginning the chart.

Switch to US 11 (8 mm) circular knitting needles and follow the chart, working rounds 8–29.

Each stitch shown in the chart should be a knit stitch. Each section of 8 stitches shown in the chart should be repeated 8 times per round.

Do not cut **Color A** or **Color B** after completing the chart, as both colors will be used in the **Crown** section.

Flash Dash Chart

Your hat should measure about 7.75" (19 cm) from the cast-on edge after you complete the chart.

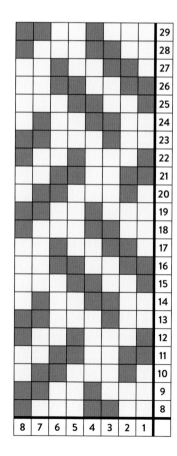

Crown

Switch to dpns or Magic Loop method (page 165) when your stitches become too tight on your needles.

You will alternate between **Color A** and **Color B** to complete the crown. Pay careful attention to the color designated for each set of stitches in each round.

Rnd 30: k2tog (**Color B**), k3 (**Color B**), k2tog (**Color A**), *k1 (**Color B**), k2tog (**Color B**), k3 (**Color B**), k2tog (**Color A**); repeat from * to last st, k1 (**Color B**). [48 sts]

Rnd 31: k2tog (**Color B**), k1 (**Color B**), k2tog (**Color A**), *k2tog (**Color B**), k2 (**Color B**), k2tog (**Color A**); repeat from * to last st, k1 (**Color B**). [32 sts]

Rnd 32: k1 (**Color B**), k2tog (**Color A**), *k2 (**Color B**), k2tog (**Color A**); repeat from * to last st, k1 (**Color B**). [24 sts]

Rnd 33: k1 (**Color B**), k1 (**Color A**), *k2tog (**Color B**), k1 (**Color A**); repeat from * to last st, then slip the last st remaining on your left needle purl-wise onto your right needle. Remove stitch marker. Now, slip the first st purl-wise from your right needle back onto your left needle and k2tog (**Color B**). Next, slip that stitch purl-wise back onto your left needle and replace the stitch marker; this stitch is now the first stitch of the next round. Cut **Color B**. [16 sts]

Rnd 34: *k2tog (**Color A**); repeat from * to end. [8 sts]

Finishing

Cut **Color A**, making sure to leave a tail roughly 12" (30 cm) long. Thread the tail through a tapestry needle and then weave it through the live stitches to take your work off your needles. Pull the tail tightly to close the top of your hat.

Weave in all remaining ends.

Give your work a gentle horizontal tug to stretch out those floats and help shape your hat. Feel free to steam block it as well!

WHIRLIGIG

I love the comfy coziness of a double brim hat, and the addition of little whirls and swirls to the brim makes it such a fun knit with a touch of whimsy! If you've never made a double brim hat before, I'll walk you through it step-by-step with this pattern—I've totally got you. Instead of a traditional, ribbed brim, this brim will be knit mostly in stockinette and then folded up and seamed together before beginning the crown to create a nice, thick, cozy layer that will feel like a warm hug around your ears.

Construction

This hat is worked in the round from the brim to the crown with a seamed double brim.

Size

One size. See the Finished Measurements section below.

This is a fitted hat designed for an adult head measuring up to 23" (58 cm). If you do not meet gauge with the suggested needles, change your needle size to meet gauge and ensure you achieve the right fit. If you prefer a snugger fit, you can size down on your needles. If you prefer a slouchier hat, you can knit extra rounds of the body before moving on to the decrease section. Any modification will affect the amount of yarn used.

Finished Measurements

Circumference: 19.75" (49 cm)

Height: 8.75" (22 cm)

Gauge

17 sts x 23 rnds = 4" (10 cm) square in stockinette and stranded pattern (brim of the hat) using US 8 (5 mm) needles

8.5 sts x 11 rnds = 2" (5 cm) square in stockinette using US 9 (5.5) mm needles

Materials

Yarn

Approximately 190 yds (174 m) total of worsted weight yarn in three contrasting colors

Color A: 140 yds (128 m)

Color B: 25 yds (23 m)

Color C: 25 yds (23 m)

Shown In

Neighborhood Fiber Co. Organic Studio Worsted (100% organic Merino wool), 200 yds (183 m) per 4 oz (114 g)

Color A: Basquiat

Color B: Waverly

Color C: Penn North

Recommended Yarn Substitution

Lion Brand Yarn Wool-Ease (80% acrylic, 20% wool), 197 yds (180 m) per 3 oz (85 g)

Suggested Needles

US 8 (5 mm) 16" (40 cm) circular knitting needles, or size needed to meet gauge

US 9 (5.5 mm) 16" (40 cm) circular knitting needles, or size needed to meet gauge

US 9 (5.5 mm) double-pointed needles or US 9 (5.5 mm) circular knitting needles with a longer cord for Magic Loop method (page 165), or size needed to meet gauge

Notions

Safety pins or straight pins (optional: for creating the double brim)

Scissors

2 stitch markers, 1 removable

Tapestry needle

Abbreviations

dpns = double-pointed needles

k = knit

k2tog = knit two together

rnd(s) = round(s)

st(s) = stitch(es)

Tips to Help You Visualize Your Project and Get You Started

*The most prominent color in this hat stems from **Color A**, so you might want to pick that color first and coordinate your other yarn with it. I loved using a variegated yarn for **Color A** and then using a couple of high-contrast colors for the little whirls and swirls on the brim.*

As a reminder, you can refer to the Colorwork Basics section (page 9) if you need help with any of the techniques used in this pattern.

PATTERN

Brim

Using US 8 (5 mm) circular knitting needles, cast on 84 sts using **Color A**. I recommend not casting on too tightly. Also, I recommend marking your first cast-on stitch with a removable stitch marker or piece of scrap yarn that will help you later when creating the double brim. Place a stitch marker and join in the round.

Rnds 1–29 (**Color A**): k to end.

Your hat should measure roughly 5" (13 cm) from the cast-on edge at this point. If it does not, just keep repeating the stockinette pattern until it does. Any modification will affect the amount of yarn used.

Cut **Color A**.

Your hat will seem wider than a hat with a ribbed brim, and that is okay! Remember, this double brim is knit mostly in stockinette stitch so it will naturally be wider when finished because it doesn't stretch as much.

Please read through all of the following notes before beginning the chart.

Work chart rounds 30–50.

Each stitch shown on the chart is a knit stitch. Each section of 12 stitches shown in the chart is repeated 7 times per round.

There are a few places where you will want to minimize the appearance of jogs by slipping the first stitch of the second round knit in your new color (see page 164 for more on jogs). These are indicated on the chart to make it easier for you.

There is also one spot where you will want to carry up **Color B**. You can do this by wrapping **Color C** (your working yarn) counterclockwise once around **Color B** (your unused yarn) and then continuing to work the chart. This also is indicated on the chart.

Cut **Color C** after round 43. Cut **Color B** after round 46.

Move on to the **Creating the Double Brim** section once you complete the chart.

Whirligig Chart

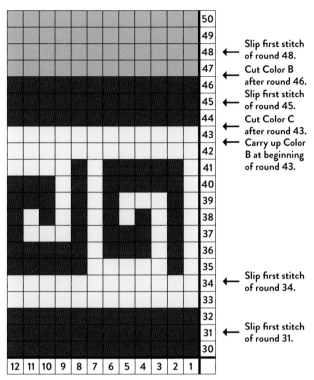

12	11	10	9	8	7	6	5	4	3	2	1	

Slip first stitch of round 48.

Cut Color B after round 46.

Slip first stitch of round 45.

Cut Color C after round 43.

Carry up Color B at beginning of round 43.

Slip first stitch of round 34.

Slip first stitch of round 31.

Color A	
Color B	
Color C	

Creating the Double Brim

There are several ways you can create a double brim for a hat. If you have a favorite method, feel free to use it! The following method described is my favorite because I like the way the seamed stitches lie smoothly on the inside.

1. Neatly weave in your cast-on tail and all other tails on the wrong side (purl side) of your work.

2. Fold the brim in half and tuck the portion with the cast-on edge up into the hat to create the inside of the double brim. About four rounds of **Color A** will create the bottom border of your double brim and be visible from the right side.

3. Line up your stitches so the first stitch of the next round matches up with the first stitch of your cast-on edge marked by your removable stitch marker. You might consider pinning both sides of the brim together to prevent it from bunching as you work, if that helps you!

4. Insert your right needle knit-wise into the first stitch of the next round on your left needle while also knit-wise picking up the front loop of the first stitch on the cast-on edge marked by your removable stitch marker. Wrap your working yarn around your needle and knit both stitches together. Remove your removable stitch marker.

5. Repeat step 4 (beginning now with the next stitch on your left needle), stitch by stitch, until you reach the end of the round. Once your double brim is completely attached, move on to the **Body** section.

Body

Switch to US 9 (5.5 mm) circular knitting needles.

Continue knitting in the round with **Color A** until your hat reaches about 7.25" (18 cm) from the bottom of the double brim before moving on to the **Crown** section.

If you prefer a bit more slouch, you can continue knitting in the round with **Color A** to your desired height before moving on to the **Crown** section. Any modifications will affect the amount of yarn used.

Crown

Switch to dpns or Magic Loop method (page 165) when your stitches become too tight on your needles.

Rnd 1: *k4, k2tog; repeat from * to end. [70 sts]

Rnd 2: K to end.

Rnd 3: *k3, k2tog; repeat from * to end. [56 sts]

Rnd 4: k to end.

Rnd 5: *k2, k2tog; repeat from * to end. [42 sts]

Rnd 6: k to end.

Rnd 7: *k1, k2tog; repeat from * to end. [28 sts]

Rnd 8: k to end.

Rnd 9: *k2tog; repeat from * to end. [14 sts]

Finishing

Cut **Color A**, making sure to leave a tail about 12" (30 cm) long. Thread the tail through a tapestry needle and then weave it through the live stitches to take your work off your needles. Pull the tail tightly to close the top of your hat.

Weave in all remaining ends.

Feel free to steam block your hat to smooth out those whirls and swirls on the cozy double brim!

TWINKLE

Look at all those diamonds in the sky! This hat would be perfect to wear on a starry night. And it would make an awesome accessory for your little stargazer as well—this pattern includes child-size instructions, too. Although I designed this hat to look like twinkling stars against a navy backdrop, you can totally put your own spin on it by choosing whatever colors you want to give it a completely different vibe—think birthday party, New Year's Eve or confetti!

Construction

This hat is worked in the round seamlessly from the brim to the crown.

Size

Measurements and information pertaining to child and adult sizes will be noted throughout this pattern as follows: Child (Adult). See the Finished Measurements section below.

This hat is designed for the average Child (Adult) head measuring up to 21 (22)"/53 (55) cm. If you do not meet gauge in the stranded pattern (main body of the hat) with the suggested needles, change your needle size to meet gauge and ensure you achieve the right fit. The sizing can also be adjusted by reducing or adding cast-on stitches in multiples of 6. Any modification will affect the amount of yarn used.

Finished Measurements

Circumference: 17.25 (19)"/43 (48) cm

Height: 8.75 (9.75)"/22 (24) cm

Gauge

13 sts = 4" (10 cm) and 7 rnds = 1.5" (4 cm) in 1 x 1 ribbing (unstretched) using US 9 (5.5 mm) needles

12.5 sts x 15 rnds = 4" (10 cm) square in the stranded pattern (main body of the hat) using US 11 (8 mm) needles

Materials

Yarn

Approximately 89 (116) yds/82 (107) m total of bulky weight yarn in two contrasting colors

Color A: 60 (84) yds/55 (77) m

Color B: 29 (32) yds/27 (30) m

Shown In

Malabrigo Yarn Chunky (100% Merino wool), 104 yds (95 m) per 3.5 oz (100 g)

Color A: Paris Night

Color B: Pollen

Recommended Yarn Substitution

Lion Brand Yarn Hue + Me (80% acrylic, 20% wool), 137 yds (125m) per 4.4 oz (125 g)

Suggested Needles

US 9 (5.5 mm) 16" (40 cm) circular knitting needles, or size needed to meet gauge

US 11 (8 mm) 16" (40 cm) circular knitting needles, or size needed to meet gauge

US 11 (8 mm) double-pointed needles or US 11 (8 mm) circular knitting needles with a longer cord for Magic Loop method (page 165), or size needed to meet gauge

Notions

Scissors

Stitch marker

Tapestry needle

*I love that the vibe of this hat can totally change with
color choice. You could even do a not-so-matchy-matchy
Mommy-and-me set with one background color for the
adult size and a different background color for the child
size while keeping the same color for both to create the
stars. Whatever you decide,* **Color A** *will be used to
create your brim and the background of your hat, so
that might be a good place for you to start! So many
fun choices for this one!*

*As a reminder, you can refer to the Colorwork Basics
section (page 9) if you need help with any of the
techniques used in this pattern.*

PATTERN

Abbreviations

dpns = double-pointed needles

k = knit

k2tog = knit two together

p = purl

rnd(s) = round(s)

st(s) = stitch(es)

Brim

Using US 9 (5.5 mm) circular knitting needles, cast
on 54 (60) sts using **Color A**. Place a stitch marker
and join in the round.

Rnds 1–7 (**Color A**): *k1, p1; repeat from * to end.

Body

Please read through all of the following notes before beginning the chart.

Switch to US 11 (8 mm) circular knitting needles and follow the chart, working rounds 8–26 (8–30).

Each stitch is a knit stitch. Each section of 6 stitches shown in the chart is repeated 9 (10) times per round.

To help minimize a jog at the join in your first large diamond, knit all the stitches in round 12 according to the chart until you get to the very last stitch of the round. Knit only the very last stitch of round 12 in **Color B**. Then, in round 13, knit only the very last stitch of the round in **Color A**.

As you begin rounds 16, 22 and 27 (for the adult version) you will want to carry up **Color B**. You can do this by wrapping **Color A** (your working yarn) counterclockwise once around **Color B** (your unused yarn) and then continuing to work the chart. I will indicate these spots for you on the chart as a friendly reminder.

Cut **Color B** after completing round 25 (29).

Your hat should measure about 6.5 (7.75)"/16 (19) cm from the cast-on edge once you complete the chart for the size you are knitting. If it does not or if you prefer more slouch, you can continue knitting in the round with **Color A** until it reaches that measurement. Any modification will affect the amount of yarn used.

If your hat measures 6.5 (7.75)"/16 (19) cm from the cast-on edge before you complete the chart, you can move on to the **Crown** section after you finish round 21 or round 24 and knit one more round in **Color A** for the child version, and after round 26 or round 28 for the adult version.

If you are knitting the child version and prefer a more fitted hat, you can move on to the **Crown** section after you finish round 21 or round 24 (depending on your desired height) and knit one more round in **Color A**. If you are knitting the adult version and prefer a more fitted hat, you can move on to the **Crown** section after you complete round 26 or round 28.

Twinkle Chart

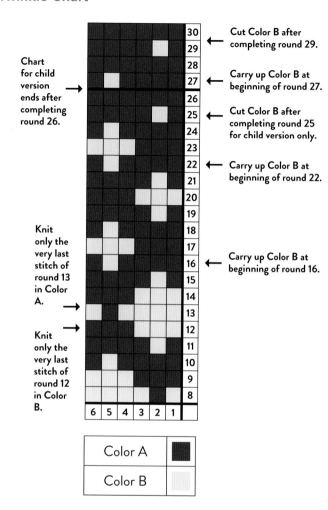

Chart for child version ends after completing round 26.

Cut Color B after completing round 29.

Carry up Color B at beginning of round 27.

Cut Color B after completing round 25 for child version only.

Carry up Color B at beginning of round 22.

Carry up Color B at beginning of round 16.

Knit only the very last stitch of round 13 in Color A.

Knit only the very last stitch of round 12 in Color B.

| Color A | ■ |
| Color B | ☐ |

Crown

Switch to dpns or Magic Loop method (page 165) when your stitches become too tight on your needles.

Use **Color A** for all remaining rounds.

Rnd 27 (31): *k4, k2tog; repeat from * to end. [45 (50) sts]

Rnd 28 (32): k to end.

Rnd 29 (33): *k3, k2tog; repeat from * to end. [36 (40) sts]

Rnd 30 (34): k to end.

Rnd 31 (35): *k2, k2tog; repeat from * to end. [27 (30) sts]

Rnd 32 (36): k to end.

Rnd 33 (37): *k1, k2tog; repeat from * to end. [18 (20) sts]

Rnd 34 (38): k to end.

Rnd 35 (39): *k2tog; repeat from * to end. [9 (10) sts]

Finishing

Cut **Color A**, making sure to leave a tail roughly 12" (30 cm) long. Thread the tail through a tapestry needle and then weave it through the live stitches to take your work off your needles. Pull the tail tightly to close the top of your hat.

Weave in all remaining ends.

Give your work a gentle horizontal tug to stretch out those floats and help shape your hat. Feel free to block it if desired.

CHECK-STRAVAGANZA

Check, check and check! Yes, please! This design offers a fun play on a traditional checkerboard pattern by creating a variety of different-sized checkerboards. Which one catches your eye first? Each time I look at the design I notice something new!

Construction

This hat is worked in the round seamlessly from the brim to the crown.

Size

One size. See the Finished Measurements section below.

This hat is designed with a bit of slouch for an adult head measuring up to 22" (55 cm). If you prefer a hat that is more fitted, there is a modification note in the **Crown** section. If you do not meet gauge in the stranded pattern (main body of the hat) with the suggested needles, change your needle size to meet gauge and ensure you achieve the right fit.

Finished Measurements

Circumference: 18.5" (46 cm)

Height: 10" (25 cm)

Gauge

13.5 sts = 4" (10 cm) and 7 rnds = 1.5" (4 cm) in 1 x 1 ribbing (unstretched) using US 9 (5.5 mm) needles

13 sts x 15 rnds = 4" (10 cm) square in the stranded pattern (main body of the hat) using US 10.5 (6.5 mm) needles

Materials

Yarn

Approximately 150 yds (138 m) total of bulky weight yarn in two contrasting colors

Color A: 76 yds (70 m)

Color B: 74 yds (68 m)

Shown In

OMG Yarn (Balls) Yosemite (100% superwash Merino wool), 120 yds (110 meters) per 3.5 oz (100 g)

Color A: Command

Color B: Girl on Fire

Recommended Yarn Substitutions

Malabrigo Yarn Chunky (100% Merino wool), 104 yds (95 m) per 3.5 oz (100 g)

Lion Brand Yarn Hue + Me (80% acrylic, 20% wool), 137 yds (125 m) per 4.4 oz (125 g)

Suggested Needles

US 9 (5.5 mm) 16" (40 cm) circular knitting needles, or size needed to meet gauge

US 10.5 (6.5 mm) 16" (40 cm) circular knitting needles, or size needed to meet gauge

US 10.5 (6.5 mm) double-pointed needles or US 10.5 (6.5 mm) circular knitting needles with a longer cord for Magic Loop method (page 165), or size needed to meet gauge

Notions

Scissors

Stitch marker

Tapestry needle

Abbreviations

dpns = double-pointed needles

k = knit

k2tog = knit two together

p = purl

rnd(s) = round(s)

st(s) = stitch(es)

Tips to Help You Visualize Your Project and Get You Started

*For this hat, you'll use **Color A** to cast on and create the brim and some of the checker pattern throughout the body. You'll use **Color B** to create your background color, some of the checkers and the crown. I recommend using solid colors for this pattern as the details of the design could get lost with variegated yarn.*

As a reminder, you can refer to the Colorwork Basics section (page 9) if you need help with any of the techniques used in this pattern.

PATTERN

Brim

Using US 9 (5.5 mm) circular knitting needles, cast on 60 sts using **Color A**. Place a stitch marker and join in the round.

Rnds 1–7 (Color A): *k1, p1; repeat from * to end.

Body

Please read through all of the following notes before beginning the chart.

Switch to US 10.5 (6.5 mm) circular knitting needles and follow the chart, working rounds 8–31.

Each stitch shown in the chart is a knit stitch. Each section of 12 stitches shown in the chart is repeated 5 times per round.

At the beginning of rounds 14 and 20 you will want to carry up **Color B**. You can do this simply by wrapping **Color A** (your working yarn) counterclockwise once around **Color B** (your unused yarn) and then continuing to work the chart. I will indicate both these spots on the chart as a friendly reminder!

Cut **Color A** after completing round 30.

Your hat should measure about 7.75" (19) cm from the cast-on edge once you complete the chart. If it does not or if you prefer more slouch, you can continue knitting in the round with **Color B** until it reaches that measurement. Any modification will affect the amount of yarn used.

Checkstravaganza Chart

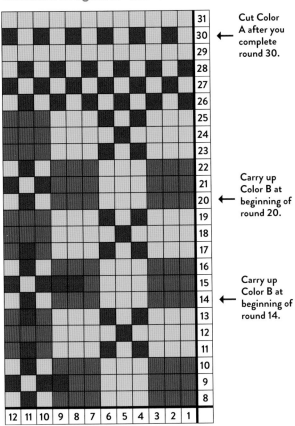

| 12 | 11 | 10 | 9 | 8 | 7 | 6 | 5 | 4 | 3 | 2 | 1 |

Cut Color A after you complete round 30. ← (round 30)

Carry up Color B at beginning of round 20. ← (round 20)

Carry up Color B at beginning of round 14. ← (round 14)

| Color A | ■ |
| Color B | ▨ |

Crown

Switch to dpns or Magic Loop method (page 165) when your stitches become too tight on your needles.

Use **Color B** for all remaining rounds.

If you prefer a hat that is more fitted, you can omit the odd-numbered knit rounds below.

Rnd 32: *k4, k2tog; repeat from * to end. [50 sts]

Rnd 33: k to end.

Rnd 34: *k3, k2tog; repeat from * to end. [40 sts]

Rnd 35: k to end.

Rnd 36: *k2, k2tog; repeat from * to end. [30 sts]

Rnd 37: k to end.

Rnd 38: *k1, k2tog; repeat from * to end. [20 sts]

Rnd 39: k to end.

Rnd 40: *k2tog; repeat from * to end. [10 sts]

Finishing

Cut **Color B**, making sure to leave a tail roughly 12" (30 cm) long. Thread the tail through a tapestry needle and then weave it through the live stitches to take your work off your needles. Pull the tail tightly to close the top of your hat.

Weave in all remaining ends.

Give your work a gentle horizontal tug to stretch out those floats and help shape your hat. Feel free to steam block it.

HOPSCOTCH

This design features simple rectangular shapes placed around the body of the hat to resemble a series of mini hopscotch games. It's so fun to watch the pattern form as you knit it up, and it also allows you to expand your skillset if you've never caught long floats before. I know the idea of catching long floats can sound scary for some, but I've got you covered with a super simple trick to help you out in the Colorwork Basics section (page 9). I hope you have so much fun with this one, continuing to play with color, as always!

Construction

This hat is worked in the round seamlessly from the brim to the crown.

Size

One size. See the Finished Measurements section below.

This hat is designed with a bit of slouch for an adult head measuring up to 22" (55 cm). If you do not meet gauge in the stranded pattern (main body of the hat) with the suggested needles, change your needle size to meet gauge and ensure you achieve the right fit.

Finished Measurements

Circumference: 17.75" (44 cm)

Height (from the bottom of the folded brim): 9.5" (24 cm)

Gauge

20 sts x 24 rnds = 4" (10 cm) square in 1 x 1 ribbing (unstretched) using US 7 (4.5 mm) needles

18 sts x 18 rnds = 4" (10 cm) square in the stranded pattern (main body of the hat) using US 9 (5.5 mm) needles

Materials

Yarn

Approximately 175 yds (160 m) total of worsted weight yarn in two contrasting colors

Color A: 136 yds (125 m)

Color B: 39 yds (36 m)

Shown In

Lion Brand Yarn Wool-Ease (80% acrylic, 20% wool), 197 yds (180 m) per 3 oz (85 g)

Color A: Canyon Sunset

Color B: Cranberry

Recommended Yarn Substitutions

Malabrigo Yarn Washted (100% superwash Merino wool), 210 yds (192 m) per 3.5 oz (100 g)

Malabrigo Yarn Worsted (100% Merino wool), 210 yds (192 m) per 3.5 oz (100 g)

Suggested Needles

US 7 (4.5 mm) 16" (40 cm) circular knitting needles, or size needed to meet gauge

US 9 (5.5 mm) 16" (40 cm) circular knitting needles, or size needed to meet gauge

US 9 (5.5 mm) double-pointed needles or US 9 (5.5 mm) circular knitting needles with a longer cord for Magic Loop method (page 165), or size needed to meet gauge

Notions

Scissors

Stitch marker

Tapestry needle

Yarn pom or faux fur pom (optional)

Abbreviations

dpns = double-pointed needles

k = knit

k2tog = knit two together

p = purl

rnd(s) = round(s)

st(s) = stitch(es)

Tips to Help You Visualize Your Project and Get You Started

Color A will be used to create the folded brim of this hat and the background color of the body, so you might want to start by choosing this color. You might find inspiration from a traditional hopscotch game drawn on blacktop with white chalk and use neutral colors, or you can dream up a colorful yarn combination with bright hues!

As a reminder, you can refer to the Colorwork Basics section (page 9) if you need help with any of the techniques used in this pattern.

PATTERN

Brim

Using US 7 (4.5 mm) circular knitting needles, cast on 80 sts using **Color A**. Place a stitch marker and join in the round.

Rnds 1–35 (**Color A**): *k1, p1; repeat from * to end.

Your brim should measure roughly 6" (15 cm) from the cast-on edge at this point, resulting in a 3" (8-cm) folded brim. If it does not, just keep repeating the 1 x 1 rib pattern until it does.

Switch to US 9 (5.5 mm) circular knitting needles.

Rnd 36 (**Color A**): k to end.

Body

Please read through all of the following notes before beginning the chart.

Work chart rounds 37–59.

All stitches shown in the chart are knit stitches. Each section of 10 stitches shown in the chart is repeated 8 times per round.

You will want to catch your **Color A** floats on all the rounds with nine consecutive **Color B** stitches. You can do this by floating the unused color (**Color A**), making sure to leave plenty of slack. Then, on the next round, when you reach the middle of the long float, pick it up with your left needle and knit it together with the next stitch. These spots will be indicated on the chart as a friendly reminder.

Cut **Color B** after completing round 58.

Hopscotch Chart

Your hat should measure about 8" (20 cm) from the bottom of the folded brim after you complete the chart. If it does not or if you prefer more slouch, you can continue to knit in the round using **Color A** until you reach the correct measurement/your desired height. Any modification will affect the amount of yarn used.

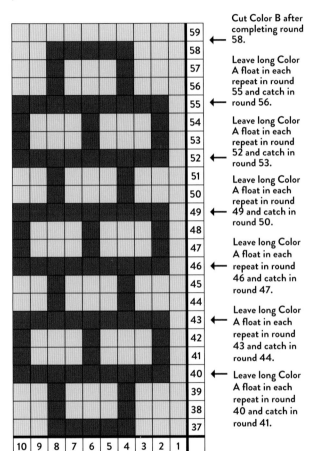

Cut Color B after completing round 58.

Leave long Color A float in each repeat in round 55 and catch in round 56.

Leave long Color A float in each repeat in round 52 and catch in round 53.

Leave long Color A float in each repeat in round 49 and catch in round 50.

Leave long Color A float in each repeat in round 46 and catch in round 47.

Leave long Color A float in each repeat in round 43 and catch in round 44.

Leave long Color A float in each repeat in round 40 and catch in round 41.

Color A	
Color B	

Crown

Switch to dpns or Magic Loop method (page 165) when your stitches become too tight on your needles.

Use **Color A** for all remaining rounds.

Rnd 60: *k6, k2tog; repeat from * to end. [70 sts]

Rnd 61: *k5, k2tog; repeat from * to end. [60 sts]

Rnd 62: *k4, k2tog; repeat from * to end. [50 sts]

Rnd 63: *k3, k2tog; repeat from * to end. [40 sts]

Rnd 64: *k2, k2tog; repeat from * to end. [30 sts]

Rnd 65: *k1, k2tog; repeat from * to end. [20 sts]

Rnd 66: *k2tog; repeat from * to end. [10 sts]

Finishing

Cut **Color A**, making sure to leave a tail about 12" (30 cm) long. Thread the tail through a tapestry needle and then weave it through the live stitches to take your work off your needles. Pull the tail tightly to close the top of your hat.

Weave in all remaining ends.

Feel free to block your hat.

BEHIND
the Scenes

Now is your chance to grab the most gorgeous variegated or tonal yarn from your stash or order that skein you've had your eye on forever. The patterns in this chapter are all designed to showcase the beauty of multi-colored yarn by using it as a backdrop for stranded silhouettes.

There is so much room to interpret each design in your own way here, my friends, and I encourage you to really bring out your inner artist and let the colors speak to you.

Blossom (page 77) features pretty, floral silhouettes just above the brim, and you can totally change the vibe of the hat simply by switching up the background color—pinks and purples for early spring and reds and oranges for fall. Bonfire (page 91) brings on all the cozy feels with a folded brim and dancing flames against a fiery, variegated backdrop that makes for a perfect fall accessory. And Taking Flight (page 101) encourages you to knit a flock of seagulls in a sky that is the color of your choice—maybe bright blue with hints of white or deep oranges and purple reminiscent of a sunrise.

Mixing variegated yarn with colorwork can totally be done, but it can also be tricky at times. The patterns in these pages let you play with all the gorgeousness of variegated yarn without the fear that the design will get lost. Feel free to experiment with unexpected colors!

Another awesome thing about these patterns is that you can knit them in the reverse color combination, using variegated yarn to create the silhouette design and a dark solid color to serve as the background. Or break the rules like an artist and use a fade of colors for an extra special, one-of-a-kind background.

BLOSSOM

I love the beauty of fresh flowers, and I designed this hat as a way to keep them with you whenever you wear it. The silhouettes of the flowers sit just above the brim to showcase your gorgeous, variegated yarn as you knit your way toward the crown. With a slightly slouchy fit, this hat is lightweight yet warm—a perfect everyday hat going into fall or spring. You can just change up the background color to reflect the season!

Construction

This hat is worked in the round seamlessly from the brim to the crown.

Size

One size. See the Finished Measurements section below.

This hat is designed with a bit of slouch for an adult head measuring up to 23" (58 cm). If you do not meet gauge in the stranded pattern (main body of the hat) with the suggested needles, change your needle size to meet gauge and ensure you achieve the right fit.

Finished Measurements

Circumference: 19" (48 cm)

Height: 10" (25 cm)

Gauge

19 sts = 4" (10 cm) and 9 rnds = 1.5" (4 cm) in 1 x 1 ribbing (unstretched) using US 7 (4.5 mm) needles

9 sts x 10 rnds = 2" (5 cm) square in the stranded pattern (main body of the hat) with US 9 (5.5 mm) needles. The main part of the flower without the bottom leaves (indicated on the chart in rounds 17-25) should fit within that 2" (5 cm) square.

Materials

Yarn

Approximately 153 yds (140 m) total of worsted weight yarn in two contrasting colors

Color A: 120 yds (110 m)

Color B: 33 yds (31 m)

Shown In

Malabrigo Yarn Mecha* (100% superwash Merino wool), 130 yds (119 m) per 3.5 oz (100 g)

*Although Mecha is listed as a bulky yarn, I found that it worked well for this pattern.

Color A: Glaze

Malabrigo Yarn Worsted (100% Merino wool), 210 yds (192 m) per 3.5 oz (100 g)

Color B: Black

Recommended Yarn Substitution

Lion Brand Yarn Basic Stitch Anti Pilling™ (100% acrylic), 185 yds (170 m) per 3.5 oz (100 g)

Suggested Needles

US 7 (4.5 mm) 16" (40 cm) circular knitting needles, or size needed to meet gauge

US 9 (5.5 mm) 16" (40 cm) circular knitting needles, or size needed to meet gauge

US 9 (5.5 mm) double-pointed needles or US 9 (5.5 mm) circular knitting needles with a longer cord for Magic Loop method (page 165), or size needed to meet gauge

Notions

Scissors

Stitch marker

Tapestry needle

Abbreviations

dpns = double-pointed needles

k = knit

k2tog = knit two together

p = purl

rnd(s) = round(s)

st(s) = stitch(es)

Tips to Help You Visualize Your Project and Get You Started

This pattern is designed to showcase all the gorgeous colors of the yarn you choose for **Color A,** *so that should definitely be your starting point. It's also meant to be a versatile pattern! You can knit one in purples or pinks for late winter/early spring to reflect the colors of the beautiful blooms to come. Or, if you're making one in the fall, you can choose yarn with a mix of yellows, oranges and reds for a perfect fall accessory!*

If you choose to use black for **Color B** *as I did, I recommend avoiding yarn with any black or black speckles in it for* **Color A** *for this specific pattern, as the design could get lost where* **Color A** *and* **Color B** *meet.*

As a reminder, you can refer to the Colorwork Basics section (page 9) if you need help with any of the techniques used in this pattern.

PATTERN

Brim

Using US 7 (4.5 mm) circular knitting needles, cast on 84 sts using **Color A**. Place a stitch marker and join in the round.

Rnd 1–9 (**Color A**): *k1, p1; repeat from * to end.

Switch to US 9 (5.5 mm) circular knitting needles.

Rnd 10 (**Color A**): k to end.

Body

Please read through all of the following notes before beginning the chart.

Work chart rounds 11–25.

All stitches shown on the chart are knit stitches. Each section of 12 stitches shown in the chart is repeated 7 times per round.

At the beginning of rounds 22 and 25, you will want to carry up **Color B**. You can do this simply by wrapping **Color A** (your working yarn) counterclock-wise once around **Color B** (your unused yarn) and then continuing to work the chart. I will indicate both these spots on the chart as a friendly reminder!

Also, as you knit the hat, there will be a few spots where you will want to catch **Color B** floats, as they tend to be too long otherwise. You can do this by floating the unused color (**Color B**), making sure to leave plenty of slack. Then, on the next round, when you reach the middle of the long float, pick it up with your left needle and knit it together with the next stitch. These spots will also be indicated on the chart.

Cut **Color B** after round 25.

Blossom Chart

Your hat should measure about 4.75" (12 cm) from the cast-on edge after completing the chart.

Once you complete the chart, continue knitting in the round with **Color A** until your hat reaches about 8.5" (21 cm) from the cast-on edge before moving on to the **Crown** section.

If you prefer a more fitted hat, you can knit fewer rounds with **Color A** after you complete the chart to your desired height before moving on to the **Crown** section. If you prefer a bit more slouch, you can continue knitting in the round with **Color A** to your desired height before moving on to the **Crown** section. Any modifications will affect the amount of yarn used.

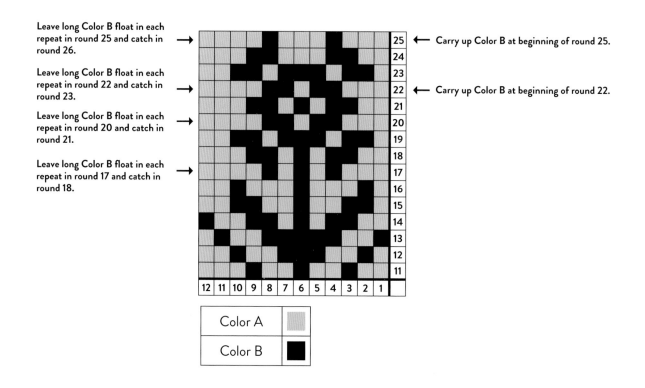

Leave long Color B float in each repeat in round 25 and catch in round 26.

Leave long Color B float in each repeat in round 22 and catch in round 23.

Leave long Color B float in each repeat in round 20 and catch in round 21.

Leave long Color B float in each repeat in round 17 and catch in round 18.

Carry up Color B at beginning of round 25.

Carry up Color B at beginning of round 22.

| Color A | |
| Color B | |

Crown

Switch to dpns or Magic Loop method (page 165) when your stitches become too tight on your needles.

Use **Color A** for all remaining rounds.

Rnd 1: *k4, k2tog; repeat from * to end. [70 sts]

Rnd 2: k to end.

Rnd 3: *k3, k2tog; repeat from * to end. [56 sts]

Rnd 4: k to end.

Rnd 5: *k2, k2tog; repeat from * to end. [42 sts]

Rnd 6: k to end.

Rnd 7: *k1, k2tog; repeat from * to end. [28 sts]

Rnd 8: k to end.

Rnd 9: *k2tog; repeat from * to end. [14 sts]

Finishing

Cut **Color A**, making sure to leave a tail about 12" (30 cm) long. Thread the tail through a tapestry needle and then weave it through the live stitches to take your work off your needles. Pull the tail tightly to close the top of your hat.

Weave in all remaining ends.

Feel free to block your hat.

SUNSET SKY

Sunsets just evoke a sense of wonder, peace and marvel for me every time. No matter what is going on, sunsets seem to put the whole world on pause and give you time to breathe and admire the natural beauty all around you. This hat is designed to give you all those feels each time you wear it. This pattern also is a perfect way to show off some of your most gorgeous tonal or variegated yarn.

Construction

This hat is worked in the round seamlessly from the brim to the crown.

Size

One size. See the Finished Measurements section below.

This is a fitted hat designed for an adult head measuring up to 22" (55 cm). If you do not meet gauge in the stranded pattern (main body of the hat) with the suggested needles, change your needle size to meet gauge and ensure you achieve the right fit.

Finished Measurements

Circumference: 17.75" (44 cm)

Height: 8.75" (22 cm)

Gauge

19 sts = 4" (10 cm) and 9 rnds = 1.25" (3 cm) in 1 x 1 ribbing (unstretched) using US 7 (4.5 mm) needles

18 sts x 23 rnds = 4" (10 cm) square in the stranded pattern (main body of the hat) using US 9 (5.5 mm) needles

Materials

Yarn

Approximately 134 yds (123 m) total of worsted weight yarn in two contrasting colors

Color A: 110 yds (101 m)

Color B: 24 yds (22 m)

Shown In

Neighborhood Fiber Co. Organic Studio Worsted (100% organic Merino wool), 200 yds (183 m) per 4 oz (114 g)

Color A: Gwynn Oak

Color B: Upton

Recommended Yarn Substitution

Lion Brand Yarn Wool-Ease (80% acrylic, 20% wool), 197 yds (180 m) per 3 oz (85 g)

Suggested Needles

US 7 (4.5 mm) 16" (40 cm) circular knitting needles, or size needed to meet gauge

US 9 (5.5 mm) 16" (40 cm) circular knitting needles, or size needed to meet gauge

US 9 (5.5 mm) double-pointed needles or US 9 (5.5 mm) circular knitting needles with a longer cord for Magic Loop method (page 165), or size needed to meet gauge

Notions

4 stitch markers (1 unique for beginning of round)

Scissors

Tapestry needle

Abbreviations

dpns = double-pointed needles

k = knit

k2tog = knit two together

p = purl

rnd(s) = round(s)

st(s) = stitch(es)

Tips to Help You Visualize Your Project and Get You Started

I love the watercolor-like stripes with blurred edges that can form as you watch a sunset. This pattern is the perfect opportunity to use any tonal yarn that can give you that same effect. A variegated or speckled yarn could also be gorgeous as a backdrop for this design. I used yarn with beautiful shades of red and orange for **Color A***, but you could also use yarn with cooler shades like purple, pink and blue—whatever image of sunset brings you the most peace and tranquility.*

If you choose to use black for **Color B** *as I did, I recommend avoiding yarn for* **Color A** *with any black or black speckles in it for this specific pattern, as the design could get lost where* **Color A** *and* **Color B** *meet.*

As a reminder, you can refer to the Colorwork Basics section (page 9) if you need help with any of the techniques used in this pattern.

PATTERN

Brim

Using US 7 (4.5 mm) circular knitting needles, cast on 80 sts using **Color A**. Place your unique stitch marker and join in the round.

Rnds 1–9 (**Color A**): *k1, p1; repeat from * to end.

Body

Switch to US 9 (5.5 mm) circular knitting needles.

Rnd 10 (**Color A**): *k20, place marker; repeat from * to end. The markers will help you better visualize the beginning and end of each repeat.

Please read through all of the following notes before beginning the chart.

Work chart rounds 11–22.

All stitches shown in the chart are knit stitches. Each section of 20 stitches is repeated 4 times per round.

At the beginning of rounds 13, 16, 18, 19, 20 and 21 you will want to carry up **Color B**. You can do this by wrapping **Color A** (your working yarn) counter-clockwise once around **Color B** (your unused yarn) and then continuing to work the chart. I will indicate these spots on the chart as a friendly reminder!

You will want to catch long floats in several spots on the chart. You can do this by floating the unused color, making sure to leave plenty of slack. Then, on the next round, when you reach the middle of the long float, pick it up with your left needle and knit it together with the next stitch. These spots also will be indicated on the chart.

Cut **Color B** after round 21.

Remove markers added in round 10 as you work round 22.

Sunset Sky Chart

Your hat should measure about 3.5" (9 cm) from the cast-on edge after completing the chart.

Once you complete the chart, continue knitting in the round with **Color A** until your hat reaches about 7.5" (19 cm) from the cast-on edge before moving on to the **Crown** section.

If you prefer a bit more slouch, you can continue knitting in the round with **Color A** to your desired height before moving on to the **Crown** section. Any modifications will affect the amount of yarn used.

Crown

Switch to dpns or Magic Loop method (page 165) when your stitches become too tight on your needles.

Use **Color A** for all remaining rounds.

Rnd 1: *k3, k2tog; repeat from * to end. [64 sts]

Rnd 2: k to end.

Rnd 3: *k2, k2tog; repeat from * to end. [48 sts]

Rnd 4: k to end.

Rnd 5: *k1, k2tog; repeat from * to end. [32 sts]

Rnd 6: k to end.

Rnd 7: *k2tog; repeat from * to end. [16 sts]

Finishing

Cut **Color A**, making sure to leave a tail about 12" (30 cm) long. Thread the tail through a tapestry needle and then weave it through the live stitches to take your work off your needles. Pull the tail tightly to close the top of your hat.

Weave in all remaining ends.

I recommend steam blocking this hat to smooth out those sunsets and showcase them in all their glory.

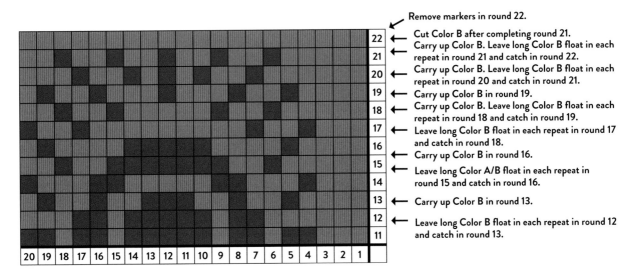

Remove markers in round 22.

22 ← Cut Color B after completing round 21.
21 ← Carry up Color B. Leave long Color B float in each repeat in round 21 and catch in round 22.
20 ← Carry up Color B. Leave long Color B float in each repeat in round 20 and catch in round 21.
19 ← Carry up Color B in round 19.
18 ← Carry up Color B. Leave long Color B float in each repeat in round 18 and catch in round 19.
17 ← Leave long Color B float in each repeat in round 17 and catch in round 18.
16 ← Carry up Color B in round 16.
15 ← Leave long Color A/B float in each repeat in round 15 and catch in round 16.
14
13 ← Carry up Color B in round 13.
12 ← Leave long Color B float in each repeat in round 12 and catch in round 13.
11

| 20 | 19 | 18 | 17 | 16 | 15 | 14 | 13 | 12 | 11 | 10 | 9 | 8 | 7 | 6 | 5 | 4 | 3 | 2 | 1 |

| Color A | |
| Color B | |

REEDS & RUSHES

I love nature, my friends, and cattails have always been an early sign of fall in the Midwest where I was born and raised. The cattails grow tall in marshy areas, and I just love how they bend and sway when the crisp, autumn wind blows. The silhouettes of those cattails will pop in this design against some beautiful, variegated yarn. This hat is such a perfect accessory to wear on a fall hike!

Construction

This hat is worked in the round seamlessly from the brim to the crown.

Size

One size. See the Finished Measurements section on the next page.

This is a slouchy hat designed for an adult head measuring up to 22" (55 cm). If you do not meet gauge in the stranded pattern (main body of the hat) with the suggested needles, change your needle size to meet gauge and ensure you achieve the right fit.

Materials

Yarn

Approximately 115 yds (106 m) total of bulky weight yarn in two contrasting colors

Color A: 84 yds (77 m) total in 4 fading colors

Color B: 31 yds (29 m)

Shown In

Jems Luxe Fibers Monster Minis (100% superwash Merino wool), 21 yds (20 m) per 0.7 oz (20 g)

Color A: Demeter's Fade in (from brim to crown) Reunited, A Mother's Love, Demeter and Crown of Grains

Jems Luxe Fibers Monstrous (100% superwash Merino wool) 106 yds (97 m) per 3.5 oz (100 g)

Color B: Jet

Recommended Yarn Substitution

Loops & Threads® Barcelona Big!™ (100% acrylic), 410 yds (375 m) per 8.8 oz (250 g)

Suggested Needles

US 10 (6 mm) 16" (40 cm) circular knitting needles, or size needed to meet gauge

US 11 (8 mm) 16" (40 cm) circular knitting needles, or size needed to meet gauge

US 11 (8 mm) double-pointed needles or US 11 (8 mm) circular knitting needles with a longer cord for Magic Loop method (page 165), or size needed to meet gauge

Notions

Scissors

Stitch marker

Tapestry needle

Finished Measurements

Circumference: 19.25" (48 cm)

Height: 10" (25 cm)

Gauge

15 sts = 4" (10 cm) and 7 rnds = 1.5" (4 cm) in 1 x 1 twisted ribbing (unstretched) using US 10 (6 mm) needles

12.5 sts x 15 rnds = 4" (10 cm) square in the stranded pattern (main body of the hat) using US 11 (8 mm) needles

Abbreviations

dpns = double-pointed needles

k = knit

k1tbl = knit one stitch through the back loop

k2tog = knit two together

p = purl

rnd(s) = round(s)

st(s) = stitch(es)

Tips to Help You Visualize Your Project and Get You Started

*This nature-inspired design gives you so many possibilities for showcasing your favorite variegated yarn. Cattails combine beautiful, rich brown and green tones, so you could choose yarn with those hues for **Color A**. Or you could pick yarn that looks like an autumn sky to make those cattail silhouettes pop against it. You might also consider a fade of various variegated yarn to create your background like I did for my sample. I used a set of bulky mini skeins that each had 21 yards (20 m), and I knit each color until I got as close to the end as comfortably possible without running out of yarn. There are so many fun options to make this beauty your own!*

*If you choose to use black for **Color B** as I did, I recommend avoiding yarn with any black or black speckles in it for **Color A** for this specific pattern, as the design could get lost where **Color A** and **Color B** meet.*

As a reminder, you can refer to the Colorwork Basics section (page 9) if you need help with any of the techniques used in this pattern.

PATTERN

Brim

Using US 10 (6 mm) circular knitting needles, cast on 60 sts using **Color A**. Place a stitch marker and join in the round.

Rnds 1–7 (**Color A**): *k1tbl, p1; repeat from * to end.

Body

Please read through all of the following notes before beginning the chart.

Switch to US 11 (8 mm) circular knitting needles and follow the chart, working rounds 8–28.

Each stitch shown in the chart is a knit stitch. Each section of 12 stitches shown in the chart is repeated 5 times per round.

In rounds 26 and 27 you will have long **Color B** floats, and you might consider catching them. You can do this by floating the unused color (**Color B**), making sure to leave plenty of slack. Then, on the next round, when you reach the middle of the long float, pick it up with your left needle and knit it together with the next stitch. I will indicate those spots on the chart as a friendly reminder if you choose to do this.

Cut **Color B** after round 27.

Reeds & Rushes Chart

Your hat should measure about 7" (18 cm) from the cast-on edge after completing the chart.

Once you complete the chart, continue knitting in the round with **Color A** until your hat reaches about 8" (20 cm) from the cast-on edge before moving on to the **Crown** section.

If you prefer a more fitted hat, you can move on to the **Crown** section right after you complete the chart. If you prefer a bit more slouch, you can continue knitting in the round with **Color A** to your desired height before moving on to the **Crown** section. Any modifications will affect the amount of yarn used.

Crown

Switch to dpns or Magic Loop method (page 165) when your stitches become too tight on your needles.

Use **Color A** for all remaining rounds.

Rnd 1: *k3, k2tog; repeat from * to end. [48 sts]

Rnd 2: k to end.

Rnd 3: *k2, k2tog; repeat from * to end. [36 sts]

Rnd 4: k to end.

Rnd 5: *k1, k2tog; repeat from * to end. [24 sts]

Rnd 6: k to end.

Rnd 7: *k2tog; repeat from * to end. [12 sts]

Finishing

Cut **Color A**, making sure to leave a tail roughly 12" (30 cm) long. Thread the tail through a tapestry needle and then weave it through the live stitches to take your work off your needles. Pull the tail tightly to close the top of your hat.

Weave in all remaining ends.

Give your work a gentle horizontal tug to stretch out those floats and help shape your hat. I steam blocked my hat to smooth out my stitches—feel free to do the same.

Chart rows (top to bottom): 28, 27, 26, 25, 24, 23, 22, 21, 20, 19, 18, 17, 16, 15, 14, 13, 12, 11, 10, 9, 8

Chart columns: 12 11 10 9 8 7 6 5 4 3 2 1

Cut Color B after completing round 27.

Leave long Color B float in each repeat in round 27 and catch in round 28.

Leave long Color B float in each repeat in round 26 and catch in round 27.

	Color A
	Color B

BONFIRE

Cozy up under a blanket beneath a sky full of stars on a crisp fall evening and let this hat bring you warmth while you make s'mores with family and friends. Or take it along as an awesome accessory for a weekend camping trip or a visit to the pumpkin patch. Wherever you decide to wear this hat, I hope the flickering flames and embers of the design keep you super toasty.

Construction

This hat is worked in the round seamlessly from the brim to the crown.

Size

One size. See the Finished Measurements section below.

This is a fitted hat designed for an adult head measuring up to 22" (55 cm). If you do not meet gauge in the stranded pattern (main body of the hat) with the suggested needles, change your needle size to meet gauge and ensure you achieve the right fit.

Finished Measurements

Circumference: 18" (45 cm)

Height (from the bottom of the folded brim): 9" (23 cm)

Gauge

16 sts x 24 rnds = 4" (10 cm) square in 1 x 1 ribbing (unstretched) using US 8 (5 mm) needles

16 sts x 19 rnds = 4" (10 cm) square in the stranded pattern (main body of the hat) using US 10 (6 mm) needles

Materials

Yarn

Approximately 142 yds (130 m) total of Aran or heavy worsted weight yarn in two contrasting colors

Color A: 125 yds (115 m)

Color B: 17 yds (16 m)

Shown In

Fully Spun Postscript Aran (100% superwash Merino wool), 177 yds (162 m) per 3.5 oz (100 g)

Color A: Sunshine

Color B: Loyal Pup

Recommended Yarn Substitution

Loops & Threads Impeccable™ (100% acrylic), 285 yds (260 m) per 4.5 oz (128 g)

Suggested Needles

US 8 (5 mm) 16" (40 cm) circular knitting needles, or size needed to meet gauge

US 10 (6 mm) 16" (40 cm) circular knitting needles, or size needed to meet gauge

US 10 (6 mm) double-pointed needles or US 10 (6 mm) circular knitting needles with a longer cord for Magic Loop method (page 165), or size needed to meet gauge

Notions

4 stitch markers, 1 unique for beginning of round

Scissors

Tapestry needle

Abbreviations

dpns = double-pointed needles

k = knit

k2tog = knit two together

p = purl

rnd(s) = round(s)

st(s) = stitch(es)

Tips to Help You Visualize Your Project and Get You Started

This hat is designed to show off the most beautiful variegated or tonal yarn you have in your stash (or have had on your wish list for the longest time). I recommend going with yarn for Color A that features gorgeous shades of yellow, orange and red to evoke that bonfire feel. But, as always, if you prefer a different vibe, you could choose yarn with purples, greens or blues to create flames with a cooler feel. It's totally up to you! Oh, and depending on your available yardage, you should be able to make another hat using the reverse color combo—win, win!

If you choose to use black for Color B as I did, I recommend avoiding yarn with any black or black speckles in it for Color A for this specific pattern, as the design could get lost where Color A and Color B meet.

As a reminder, you can refer to the Colorwork Basics section (page 9) if you need help with any of the techniques used in this pattern.

PATTERN

Brim

Using US 8 (5 mm) circular knitting needles, cast on 72 sts using **Color A**. Place your unique stitch marker and join in the round.

Rnds 1–35 (**Color A**): *k1, p1; repeat from * to end.

Your brim should measure roughly 6" (15 cm) from the cast-on edge at this point, resulting in a 3" (8-cm) folded brim. If it does not, just keep repeating the 1 x 1 rib pattern until it does.

Body

Switch to US 10 (6 mm) circular knitting needles.

Rnd 36 (**Color A**): *k18, place marker; repeat from * to end. The markers will help you better visualize the beginning and end of each repeat.

Please read through all of the following notes before beginning the chart.

Work chart rounds 37–54.

Each stitch shown on the chart is a knit stitch. Each section of 18 stitches shown in the chart is repeated 4 times per round.

Just like flames, this design is a bit fluid, and the pattern isn't as visibly apparent as others as you knit. So be sure to keep your focus on each round of that chart throughout the colorwork section and you'll be just fine!

At the beginning of round 40, you will want to carry up **Color A**. You can do this by wrapping **Color B** (your working yarn) counterclockwise once around **Color A** (your unused yarn) and then continuing to work the chart. At the beginning of rounds 43, 47 and 51 you will want to carry up **Color B**. You can do this by wrapping **Color A** counterclockwise once around **Color B** (your unused yarn) and then continuing to work the chart. I will indicate these spots on the chart as a friendly reminder!

Also, as you knit the hat, there will be a few spots where you will want to catch **Color B** floats as they tend to be too long otherwise. You can do this by floating the unused color (**Color B**), making sure to leave plenty of slack. Then, on the next round, when you reach the middle of the long float, pick it up with your left needle and knit it together with the next stitch. These spots also will be indicated on the chart.

Cut **Color B** after completing round 53.

Remove markers added in round 36 as you work round 54.

Bonfire Chart

Your hat should measure roughly 6.75" (17 cm) from the bottom of the folded brim after you complete the chart.

Once you complete the chart, continue knitting in the round with **Color A** until your hat reaches about 8" (20 cm) from the bottom of the folded brim before moving on to the **Crown** section.

If you prefer a bit more slouch, you can continue knitting in the round with **Color A** to your desired height before moving on to the **Crown** section. Any modifications will affect the amount of yarn used.

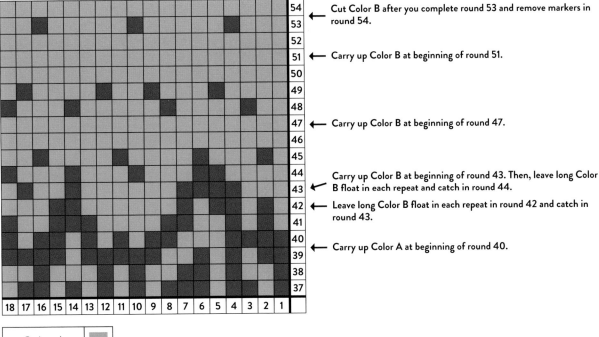

Cut Color B after you complete round 53 and remove markers in round 54.

Carry up Color B at beginning of round 51.

Carry up Color B at beginning of round 47.

Carry up Color B at beginning of round 43. Then, leave long Color B float in each repeat and catch in round 44.

Leave long Color B float in each repeat in round 42 and catch in round 43.

Carry up Color A at beginning of round 40.

| Color A | |
| Color B | |

Crown

Switch to dpns or Magic Loop method (page 165) when your stitches become too tight on your needles.

Use **Color A** for all remaining rounds.

Rnd 1: *k4, k2tog; repeat from * to end. [60 sts]

Rnd 2: k to end.

Rnd 3: *k3, k2tog; repeat from * to end. [48 sts]

Rnd 4: k to end.

Rnd 5: *k2, k2tog; repeat from * to end. [36 sts]

Rnd 6: k to end.

Rnd 7: *k1, k2tog; repeat from * to end. [24 sts]

Rnd 8: k to end.

Rnd 9: *k2tog; repeat from * to end. [12 sts]

Finishing

Cut **Color A**, making sure to leave a tail roughly 12" (30 cm) long. Thread the tail through a tapestry needle and then weave it through the live stitches to take your work off your needles. Pull the tail tightly to close the top of your hat.

Weave in all remaining ends.

Give your work a gentle horizontal tug to stretch out those floats and help shape your hat. Feel free to block it.

SEE THE FOREST

This pattern was inspired by nature and the famous expression that sometimes we "can't see the forest for the trees." Instead of variegated yarn, this design uses at least two colors held double to create the background. The marled effect doesn't show its full glory until you finish the hat, step back, allow yourself to breathe . . . and see the forest.

Construction

This hat is worked in the round seamlessly from the brim to the crown.

Size

One size. See the Finished Measurements section on the next page.

This is a fitted hat designed for an adult head measuring up to 22" (55 cm). If you do not meet gauge in the stranded pattern (main body of the hat) with the suggested needles, change your needle size to meet gauge and ensure you achieve the right fit.

Materials

Yarn

Approximately 194 yds (178 m) total of worsted weight yarn in at least two colors (held double)

Color A: 97 yds (89 m)

Color B: 97 yds (89 m)

Approximately 23 yds (21 m) total of bulky weight yarn in a color that contrasts from the worsted weight yarns

Color C: 23 yds (21 m)

I highly encourage you to knit a swatch before beginning your hat to make sure the two strands of worsted yarn you choose are comparable to the thickness of the bulky yarn you use.

Shown In

Malabrigo Yarn Worsted (100% Merino wool), 210 yds (192 m) per 3.5 oz (100 g)

Color A: Verde Adriana

Color B: Sapphire Green, Lettuce and Apple Green (faded from brim to crown)

Malabrigo Yarn Chunky (100% Merino wool), 104 yds (95 m) per 3.5 oz (100 g)

Color C: Black

Recommended Yarn Substitutions

Lion Brand Yarn Wool-Ease (80% acrylic, 20% wool), 197 yds (180 m) per 3 oz (85 g)

Lion Brand Yarn Hue + Me (80% acrylic, 20% wool), 137 yds (125 m) per 4.4 oz (125 g)

Suggested Needles

US 9 (5.5 mm) 16" (40 cm) circular knitting needles, or size needed to meet gauge

US 10.5 (6.5 mm) 16" (40 cm) circular knitting needle, or size needed to meet gauge

US 10.5 (6.5 mm) double-pointed needles or US 10.5 (6.5 mm) circular knitting needles with a longer cord for Magic Loop method (page 165), or size needed to meet gauge

Notions

Scissors

Stitch marker

Tapestry needle

Finished Measurements

Circumference: 18.25" (46 cm)

Height: 9" (23 cm)

Gauge

15 sts = 4" (10 cm) and 7 rnds = 1.25" (3 cm) in 1 x 1 twisted ribbing (unstretched) using US 9 (5.5 mm) needles

14 sts x 18 rnds = 4" (10 cm) square in the stranded and stockinette pattern (main body of the hat) using US 10.5 (6.5 mm) needles

Abbreviations

dpns = double-pointed needles

k = knit

k1tbl = knit one stitch through the back loop

k2tog = knit two together

p = purl

rnd(s) = round(s)

st(s) = stitch(es)

- -

Tips to Help You Visualize Your Project and Get You Started

This design gives you an awesome opportunity to mix different colors and create your own marled background to make those trees pop. I've found the technique of using two colors held double to be such a fun way to mimic a variegated yarn if you don't have any on hand. And if you fade the colors of yarn held double as you go, it also makes for a great stash-busting project because you can use up those small amounts of yarn you're not sure what to do with otherwise. For my sample, I held one background color throughout and mixed in other colors as I knit, using one color for the brim, a second for most of the stranded section and a third color in the last round of the stranded pattern through the crown. I stuck with shades of green, but maybe you're inspired to create a wintry scene with icy blue hues for your background. Just dive into that stash and listen to what speaks to you!

*If you choose to use black for **Color C** as I did, I recommend avoiding yarn with any black or black speckles in the other colors you select for this specific pattern, as the design could get lost where the colors meet.*

As a reminder, you can refer to the Colorwork Basics section (page 9) if you need help with any of the techniques used in this pattern.

PATTERN

Brim

Using US 9 (5.5 mm) circular knitting needles, cast on 64 sts using **Colors A and B** held double. Place a stitch marker and join in the round.

Rnds 1–7 (**Colors A and B** held double): *k1tbl, p1; repeat from * to end.

Body

Please read through all of the following notes before beginning the chart.

Switch to US 10.5 (6.5 mm) circular knitting needles and follow the chart, working rounds 8–22.

Each stitch shown in the chart is a knit stitch. Each section of 16 stitches shown in the chart is repeated 4 times per round.

In rounds 8, 10, 11, 13 and 14 you will have long **Color A** and **Color B** floats. In rounds 20 and 21 you will have long **Color C** floats. I recommend catching these floats. You can do this by floating the unused color(s), making sure to leave plenty of slack. Then, on the next round, when you reach the middle of the long float, pick up the strand(s) of the float with your left needle and knit it (them) together with the next stitch. I will indicate those spots on the chart as a friendly reminder if you choose to use this method. As always, use whatever method of catching floats works best for you!

Cut **Color C** after round 21.

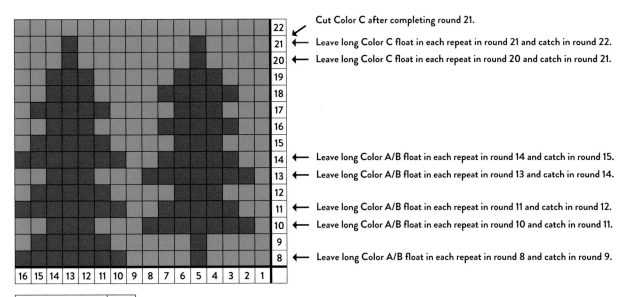

16	15	14	13	12	11	10	9	8	7	6	5	4	3	2	1		

Cut Color C after completing round 21.

← Leave long Color C float in each repeat in round 21 and catch in round 22.

← Leave long Color C float in each repeat in round 20 and catch in round 21.

← Leave long Color A/B float in each repeat in round 14 and catch in round 15.

← Leave long Color A/B float in each repeat in round 13 and catch in round 14.

← Leave long Color A/B float in each repeat in round 11 and catch in round 12.

← Leave long Color A/B float in each repeat in round 10 and catch in round 11.

← Leave long Color A/B float in each repeat in round 8 and catch in round 9.

Colors A and B	
Color C	

See the Forest Chart

Your hat should measure roughly 4.5" (11 cm) from the cast-on edge after you finish the chart.

Once you complete the chart, continue knitting in the round with **Colors A and B** held double until your hat reaches about 7.5" (19 cm) from the cast-on edge before moving on to the **Crown** section.

If you prefer a bit more slouch, you can continue knitting in the round with **Colors A and B** held double to your desired height before moving on to the **Crown** section. Any modifications will affect the amount of yarn used.

Crown

Switch to dpns or Magic Loop method (page 165) when your stitches become too tight on your needles.

Use **Colors A and B** held double for all remaining rounds.

Rnd 1: *k2, k2tog; repeat from * to end. [48 sts]

Rnd 2: k to end.

Rnd 3: *k1, k2tog; repeat from * to end. [32 sts]

Rnd 4: k to end.

Rnd 5: *k2tog; repeat from * to end. [16 sts]

Rnd 6: k to end.

Rnd 7: *k2tog; repeat from * to end. [8 sts]

Finishing

Cut **Colors A and B**, making sure to leave tails roughly 12" (30 cm) long. Thread the tails through a tapestry needle and then weave them through the live stitches to take your work off your needles. Pull the tails tightly to close the top of your hat.

Weave in all remaining ends.

Give your work a gentle horizontal tug to stretch out those floats and help shape your hat. I steam blocked my hat to smooth out my stitches—feel free to do the same.

TAKING FLIGHT

I designed this hat to represent the silhouette of a flock of gulls flying just above the horizon along the water. The pattern embodies the calm and serenity I've felt every time I've visited the ocean or walked along a lake, and I hope it gives you those same peaceful feels. Pick your favorite tonal or variegated yarn in shades of blue or teal and get to knitting! This hat would make the perfect accessory for brisk walks near the water or anytime you want to feel like you're close to a beautiful beach surrounded by the sound of waves and birds soaring over your head.

Construction

This hat is worked in the round seamlessly from the brim to the crown.

Size

One size. See the Finished Measurements section on the next page.

This hat is designed with a bit of slouch for an adult head measuring up to 22" (55 cm). If you do not meet gauge in the stranded pattern (main body of the hat) with the suggested needles, change your needle size to meet gauge and ensure you achieve the right fit. If you prefer even more slouch or a more fitted hat, modifications can be found later in this pattern. Any modification will affect the amount of yarn used.

Materials

Yarn

Approximately 139 yds (128 m) total of bulky weight yarn in two contrasting colors

Color A: 101 yds (93 m)

Color B: 38 yds (35 m)

Shown In

Malabrigo Yarn Mecha (100% superwash Merino wool), 130 yds (119 m) per 3.5 oz (100 g)

Color A: Thereza

Malabrigo Yarn Worsted* (100% Merino wool), 210 yds (192 m) per 3.5 oz (100 g)

*Although Worsted is a worsted weight yarn, I found that it worked well for this pattern.

Color B: Black

Recommended Yarn Substitution

Loops & Threads Barcelona Big! (100% acrylic), 410 yds (375 m) per 8.8 oz (250 g)

Suggested Needles

US 9 (5.5 mm) 16" (40 cm) circular knitting needles, or size needed to meet gauge

US 10.5 (6.5 mm) 16" (40 cm) circular knitting needles, or size needed to meet gauge

US 10.5 (6.5 mm) double-pointed needles or US 10.5 (6.5 mm) circular knitting needles with a longer cord for Magic Loop method (page 165), or size needed to meet gauge

Notions

3 stitch markers, 1 unique for beginning of round

Scissors

Tapestry needle

Finished Measurements

Circumference: 18" (45 cm)

Height: 9.5" (24 cm)

Gauge

18.5 sts = 4" (10 cm) and 9 rnds = 1.5" (4 cm) in 1 x 1 twisted ribbing (unstretched) using US 9 (5.5 mm) needles

8 sts x 9.5 rnds = 2" (5 cm) square in the stranded and stockinette pattern (main body of the hat) with US 10.5 (6.5 mm) needles

Abbreviations

dpns = double-pointed needles

k = knit

k1tbl = knit one stitch through the back loop

k2tog = knit two together

p = purl

rnd(s) = round(s)

st(s) = stitch(es)

Tips to Help You Visualize Your Project and Get You Started

I chose a pale blue tonal yarn as my background for this hat to symbolize water and make those silhouettes of the flying birds stand out. You could do the same, or even go with a variegated yarn with shades of teal, purple or green. And, psst! Do you see bats in this design instead of gulls? It's okay, I can totally see that, too! Just switch up your background color to a variegated orange yarn and you've got a perfect hat for Halloween. There are tons of options with this baby!

*If you choose to use black for **Color B** as I did, I recommend avoiding yarn with any black or black speckles in it for **Color A** for this specific pattern, as the design could get lost where **Color A** and **Color B** meet.*

As a reminder, you can refer to the Colorwork Basics section (page 9) if you need help with any of the techniques used in this pattern.

PATTERN

Brim

Using US 9 (5.5 mm) circular knitting needles, cast on 72 sts using **Color A**. Place your unique stitch marker and join in the round.

Rnds 1–9 (**Color A**): *k1tbl, p1; repeat from * to end.

Body

Switch to US 10.5 (6.5 mm) circular knitting needles.

Rnds 10–15 (**Color A**): k to end.

Rnd 16 (**Color A**): *k24, place marker; repeat from * to end. The markers will help you better visualize the beginning and end of each repeat.

Please read through all of the following notes before beginning the chart.

Work chart rounds 17–30.

All stitches shown on the chart are knit stitches. Each section of 24 stitches shown in the chart is repeated 3 times per round.

As you knit the hat, there will be a few spots where you will want to catch long **Color A** and **Color B** floats. You can do this by floating the unused color, making sure to leave plenty of slack. Then, on the next round, when you reach the middle of the long float, pick it up with your left needle and knit it together with the next stitch. These spots will be indicated on the chart as a friendly reminder.

To help minimize a jog at the join in one of the birds at the top of the chart, knit all the stitches in round 29 according to the chart until you get to the very last stitch of the round. Knit **only the very last stitch** of round 29 in **Color B**. Then, in round 30, knit **only the very last stitch** of the round in **Color A**. This will also be indicated on the chart for you.

Cut **Color B** after round 30.

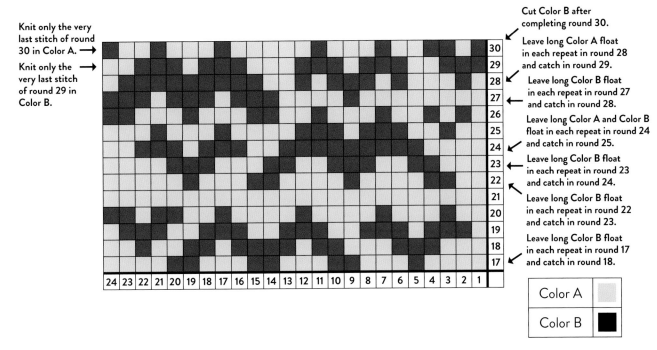

Knit only the very last stitch of round 30 in Color A. →

Knit only the very last stitch of round 29 in Color B.

Cut Color B after completing round 30.

Leave long Color A float in each repeat in round 28 and catch in round 29.

Leave long Color B float in each repeat in round 27 and catch in round 28.

Leave long Color A and Color B float in each repeat in round 24 and catch in round 25.

Leave long Color B float in each repeat in round 23 and catch in round 24.

Leave long Color B float in each repeat in round 22 and catch in round 23.

Leave long Color B float in each repeat in round 17 and catch in round 18.

| Color A | |
| Color B | |

Taking Flight Chart

Your hat should measure about 5.75" (14 cm) from the cast-on edge after completing the chart.

Once you complete the chart, continue knitting in the round with **Color A** (removing markers placed in round 16 as you knit) until your hat reaches about 7.75" (19 cm) from the cast-on edge before moving on to the **Crown** section.

If you prefer a more fitted hat, you can knit fewer rounds with **Color A** after you complete the chart to your desired height before moving on to the **Crown** section. If you prefer a bit more slouch, you can continue knitting in the round with **Color A** to your desired height before moving on to the **Crown** section. Any modifications will affect the amount of yarn used.

Crown

Switch to dpns or Magic Loop method (page 165) when your stitches become too tight on your needles.

Use **Color A** for all remaining rounds.

Rnd 1: *k4, k2tog; repeat from * to end. [60 sts]

Rnd 2: k to end.

Rnd 3: *k3, k2tog; repeat from * to end. [48 sts]

Rnd 4: k to end.

Rnd 5: *k2, k2tog; repeat from * to end. [36 sts]

Rnd 6: k to end.

Rnd 7: *k1, k2tog; repeat from * to end. [24 sts]

Rnd 8: k to end.

Rnd 9: *k2tog; repeat from * to end. [12 sts]

Finishing

Cut **Color A**, making sure to leave a tail about 12" (30 cm) long. Thread the tail through a tapestry needle and then weave it through the live stitches to take your work off your needles. Pull the tail tightly to close the top of your hat.

Weave in all remaining ends.

I highly recommend steam blocking your hat.

POPPING
Colors

If you love to knit with *all* the colors, you've come to the right place, my friends! This chapter is filled with patterns that are designed to let you be as adventurous as you like with your color palette.

The patterns you'll find in this chapter are intended to give you plenty of options, helping to ease you into incorporating more colors into your knitting. You'll find some patterns that let you decide whether to keep it simple with two colors or dive into that stash and knit up a piece with six colors. And if you prefer working within a more fixed framework, there are other designs that call for a specific number of colors.

Carousel (page 111) combines four contrasting colors to create a whimsical design that continues all the way up through the crown to give your hat that wow factor. Myriad (page 121) encourages you to experiment with up to six colors or as few as two in customizable sections—it all depends on what your inner artist is whispering to you. And in Glow (page 125), three colors radiate from the center of a series of squares to form an eye-catching design with so many possibilities for color combinations.

Remember, you're the artist and you get to fill up your palette with whatever colors you want. With so many options to choose from in these pages and so much room for customization within each pattern, you can create your own work of art that is just right for you.

PYRAMID POP

Skill Level: Easy

This hat features triangular shapes in a mix of sizes and positions throughout the pattern. Although you'll be using up to five colors, you'll only work with two contrasting colors at a time for each section. This gives you an awesome opportunity to begin working with a bunch of colors without overwhelming yourself with having to knit with all of them at once. I'm all about easing you in, my friends. Have fun making those pyramids pop whether you choose bright colors or neutrals!

Construction

This hat is worked in the round seamlessly from the brim to the crown.

Size

One size. See the Finished Measurements section on the next page.

This hat is designed with a bit of slouch for an adult head measuring up to 22" (55 cm). If you do not meet gauge in the stranded pattern (main body of the hat) with the suggested needles, change your needle size to meet gauge and ensure you achieve the right fit.

Materials

Yarn

Approximately 105 yds (97 m) total of bulky weight yarn in five contrasting colors

Color A: 21 yds (20 m)

Color B: 21 yds (20 m)

Color C: 21 yds (20 m)

Color D: 21 yds (20 m)

Color E: 21 yds (20 m)

Shown In

Jems Luxe Fibers Monster Mini (100% superwash Merino wool), 21 yds (20 m) per 0.7 oz (20 g)

Color A: Apple of Discord

Color B: Smithsonite

Color C: Pezzottaite

Color D: Serpent Slayer

Color E: Aphrodite

Recommended Yarn Substitution

Malabrigo Yarn Chunky (100% Merino wool), 104 yds (95 m) per 3.5 oz (100 g)

Suggested Needles

US 10 (6 mm) 16" (40 cm) circular knitting needles, or size needed to meet gauge

US 11 (8 mm) 16" (40 cm) circular knitting needles, or size needed to meet gauge

US 11 (8 mm) double-pointed needles or US 11 (8 mm) circular knitting needles with a longer cord for Magic Loop method (page 165), or size needed to meet gauge

Notions

Scissors

Stitch marker

Tapestry needle

Finished Measurements

Circumference: 19" (48 cm)

Height: 9.5" (24 cm)

Gauge

14 sts = 4" (10 cm) and 7 rnds = 1.5" (4 cm) in 1 x 1 ribbing (unstretched) using US 10 (6 mm) needles

12.5 sts x 16 rnds = 4" (10 cm) square in the stranded pattern (main body of the hat) using US 11 (8 mm) needles

Abbreviations

dpns = double-pointed needles

k = knit

k2tog = knit two together

p = purl

rnd(s) = round(s)

st(s) = stitch(es)

Tips to Help You Visualize Your Project and Get You Started

*I hope you have so much fun picking colors for this baby! I loved incorporating the pink yarn with speckles as my **Color E** to give it an extra pop. Just make sure as you switch from section to section that a high contrast remains between colors. If you want to stick to four colors, you can use the same color for **Color A** and **Color B**. That will alter the appearance of the bottom of the hat a bit as it won't have a contrasting stripe above the brim, but it will totally make it your own!*

As a reminder, you can refer to the Colorwork Basics section (page 9) if you need help with any of the techniques used in this pattern.

PATTERN

Brim

Using US 10 (6 mm) circular knitting needles, cast on 60 sts using **Color A**. Place a stitch marker and join in the round.

Rnds 1–7 (**Color A**): *k1, p1; repeat from * to end.

Rnd 8 (**Color A**): k to end.

Body

Please read through all of the following notes before beginning the chart.

Switch to US 11 (8 mm) circular knitting needles and follow the chart, working rounds 9–31.

Each stitch shown in the chart is a knit stitch. Each section of 12 stitches shown in the chart is repeated 5 times per round.

I cut my colors after the last round in each section. I will indicate these spots on the chart if you choose to do the same.

In round 18, you will have long **Color B** floats to carry behind your **Color E** stitches in each repeat. I recommend catching those floats. You can do this by floating the unused color (**Color B**), making sure to leave plenty of slack. Then, on the next round, when you reach the middle of the long float, pick it up with your left needle and knit it together with the next stitch. This will be indicated on the chart as a friendly reminder!

As you begin round 19, you will want to carry up **Color E**. You can do this simply by wrapping **Color B** (your working yarn) counterclockwise once around **Color E** (your unused yarn) and then continuing to work the chart. As you begin round 28, you will want to carry up **Color C**. Wrap **Color D** (your working yarn) counterclockwise once around **Color C** (your unused yarn) and then continue to work the chart. These spots also will be indicated on the chart.

Your hat should measure about 7.25" (18) cm from the cast-on edge once you complete the chart. If it does not or if you prefer more slouch, you can continue knitting in the round with **Color E** until it reaches that measurement/your desired height. Any modification will affect the amount of yarn used.

Pyramid Pop Chart

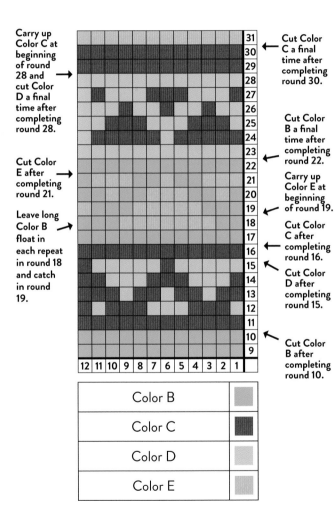

Crown

Switch to dpns or Magic Loop method (page 165) when your stitches become too tight on your needles.

Use **Color E** for all remaining rounds.

Rnd 32: *k4, k2tog; repeat from * to end. [50 sts]

Rnd 33: k to end.

Rnd 34: *k3, k2tog; repeat from * to end. [40 sts]

Rnd 35: k to end.

Rnd 36: *k2, k2tog; repeat from * to end. [30 sts]

Rnd 37: k to end.

Rnd 38: *k1, k2tog; repeat from * to end. [20 sts]

Rnd 39: k to end.

Rnd 40: *k2tog; repeat from * to end. [10 sts]

Finishing

Cut **Color E**, making sure to leave a tail roughly 12" (30 cm) long. Thread the tail through a tapestry needle and then weave it through the live stitches to take your work off your needles. Pull the tail tightly to close the top of your hat.

Weave in all remaining ends.

Give your work a gentle horizontal tug to stretch out those floats and help shape your hat. Feel free to block it.

CAROUSEL

This hat makes me want to eat some freshly spun cotton candy and ride a roller coaster. Are you with me? So many colors and varying patterns build up from the cozy cuffed brim and are capped off by a colorful crown that reminds me of the top of a carousel ride. So. Much. Fun!

Construction

This hat is worked in the round seamlessly from the brim to the crown.

Size

One size. See the Finished Measurements below.

This hat is designed with a bit of slouch for an adult head measuring up to 23" (58 cm). If you do not meet gauge in the stranded pattern (main body of the hat) with the suggested needles, change your needle size to meet gauge and ensure you achieve the right fit.

Finished Measurements

Circumference: 20" (50 cm)

Height (from the bottom of the folded brim): 10" (25 cm)

Gauge

21 sts x 22 rnds = 4" (10 cm) square in 1 x 1 ribbing (unstretched) using US 7 (4.5 mm) needles

17 sts x 21 rnds = 4" (10 cm) square in the stranded pattern (main body of the hat) using US 9 (5.5 mm) needles

Materials

Yarn

Approximately 177 yds (162 m) total of worsted weight yarn in four contrasting colors

Color A: 86 yds (79 m)

Color B: 29 yds (27 m)

Color C: 37 yds (34 m)

Color D: 25 yds (23 m)

Shown In

Lion Brand Yarn Basic Stitch Anti-Pilling (100% acrylic), 185 yds (170 m) per 3.5 oz (100 g)

Color A: Mustard

Color B: Hot Pink

Color C: Grass

Color D: Pumpkin

Recommended Yarn Substitution

Lion Brand Yarn Wool-Ease (80% acrylic, 20% wool), 197 yds (180 m) per 3 oz (85 g)

Suggested Needles

US 7 (4.5 mm) 16" (40 cm) circular knitting needles, or size needed to meet gauge

US 9 (5.5 mm) 16" (40 cm) circular knitting needles, or size needed to meet gauge

US 9 (5.5 mm) double-pointed needles or US 9 (5.5 mm) circular knitting needles with a longer cord for Magic Loop method (page 165), or size needed to meet gauge

Notions

Scissors

Stitch marker

Tapestry needle

Abbreviations

dpns = double-pointed needles

k = knit

k2tog = knit two together

p = purl

rnd(s) = round(s)

st(s) = stitch(es)

Tips to Help You Visualize Your Project and Get You Started

*Are you ready for some fun, my friends? It's time to pick your colors! This hat features a pretty even balance of colors after the brim, so you might want to start by choosing your brim color (**Color A**) and go from there. You'll work with two contrasting colors at a time for each section as you knit. Just make sure the contrast remains as you switch from section to section. For example, in the sample I knit, I wanted the green to be next to the pink instead of having the orange next to the pink because there was more contrast.*

As a reminder, you can refer to the Colorwork Basics section (page 9) if you need help with any of the techniques used in this pattern.

PATTERN

Brim

Using US 7 (4.5 mm) circular knitting needles, cast on 84 sts using **Color A**. Place a stitch marker and join in the round.

Rnds 1–32 (**Color A**): *k1, p1; repeat from * to end.

Your brim should measure roughly 6" (15 cm) from the cast-on edge at this point, resulting in a 3" (8-cm) cuffed brim. If it does not, just keep repeating the 1 x 1 rib pattern until it does.

Body

Please read through all of the following notes before beginning the chart.

Switch to US 9 (5.5 mm) circular knitting needles and follow the chart, working rounds 33–59.

All stitches shown in the chart are knit stitches. Each section of 4 stitches is repeated 21 times per round.

As I worked through the chart, I carried up my yarn along the inside of my hat in some cases. To carry up your yarn, you can wrap your working yarn counterclockwise once around your unused yarn at the beginning of the round and then continue to work the chart. In spots where there was too much space until I began working with a color again, I cut my yarn. I will indicate those spots on the chart for you if you choose to use the same method. As always, use whatever method works best for you, my friends!

At two spots in the chart, the very last stitches of rounds 43 and 44 will be knit in a different color to minimize the appearance of a jog in your pattern. These spots will be indicated on the chart to help you out.

Cut **Color A** after round 50. Cut **Color B** after you complete round 51.

You also may want to minimize the appearance of jogs in your stripes toward the top of the hat by following the steps below (see page 164 for more on jogs):

Knit your first round of stripes using **Color C** as called for in the chart. Once you reach the end of the round, remove your stitch marker. Insert your right needle purl-wise into the right leg of the **Color B** stitch below the first **Color C** stitch on your left needle. Then, using your right needle, move that **Color B** stitch up onto your left needle so it is next to the **Color C** stitch. Knit those two stitches together. Replace your stitch marker. This will shift the beginning of your round to the left by one stitch and that is totally okay! (In subsequent rounds, **Color B** will be replaced by **Color D** as you work through the stripes.)

Knit your next round of stripes in **Color D** as called for in the chart. Once you reach the end of the round, remove your stitch marker. Insert your right needle purl-wise into the right leg of the **Color C** stitch below the first **Color D** stitch on your left needle. Then, using your right needle, move that **Color C** stitch up onto your left needle so it is next to the **Color D** stitch. Knit those two stitches together. Replace your stitch marker. Again, the beginning of your round will shift to the left by one stitch, and this is okay!

Repeat both steps as you work through the stripes on the crown.

Carousel Chart

Your hat should measure 8.25" (21 cm) from the bottom of your folded brim after finishing the chart. If it does not, or if you would prefer a bit more slouch, continue repeating rounds 58 and 59 until you reach that measurement/your desired height before moving on to the **Crown** section. Any modification will affect the amount of yarn used.

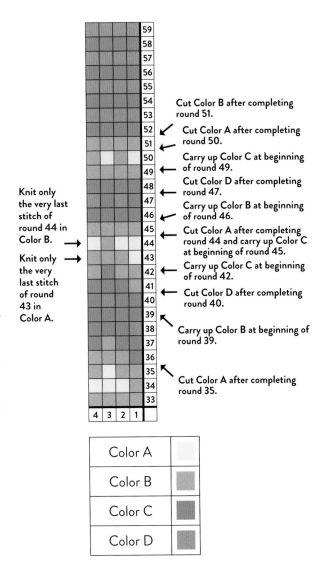

Cut Color B after completing round 51.

Cut Color A after completing round 50.

Carry up Color C at beginning of round 49.

Cut Color D after completing round 47.

Carry up Color B at beginning of round 46.

Cut Color A after completing round 44 and carry up Color C at beginning of round 45.

Carry up Color C at beginning of round 42.

Cut Color D after completing round 40.

Carry up Color B at beginning of round 39.

Cut Color A after completing round 35.

Knit only the very last stitch of round 44 in Color B.

Knit only the very last stitch of round 43 in Color A.

	Color A	
	Color B	
	Color C	
	Color D	

Crown

Switch to dpns or Magic Loop method (page 165) when your stitches become too tight on your needles.

You will alternate between **Color C** and **Color D** for the remaining rounds. Pay careful attention to the color designated for each set of stitches in each round.

Rnd 60: *k4 (**Color D**), k2tog (**Color C**); repeat from * to end. [70 sts]

Rnd 61: *k4 (**Color D**), k1 (**Color C**); repeat from * to end.

Rnd 62: *k3 (**Color D**), k2tog (**Color C**); repeat from * to end. [56 sts]

Rnd 63: *k3 (**Color D**), k1 (**Color C**); repeat from * to end.

Rnd 64: *k2 (**Color D**), k2tog (**Color C**); repeat from * to end. [42 sts]

Rnd 65: *k2 (**Color D**), k1 (**Color C**); repeat from * to end.

Rnd 66: *k1 (**Color D**), k2tog (**Color C**); repeat from * to end. [28 sts]

Rnd 67: *k1 (**Color D**), k1 (**Color C**); repeat from * to end.

Rnd 68: *k2tog (**Color C**); repeat from * to end. [14 sts]

Finishing

Cut **Color C** and **Color D**, making sure to leave tails about 12" (30 cm) long. Thread the tails through a tapestry needle and then weave them through the live stitches to take your work off your needles. Pull the tails tightly to close the top of your hat.

Weave in all remaining ends.

Feel free to block your hat.

MIRROR

This pattern is designed to keep your interest from start to finish because it's only when you're done knitting that you'll see the full effect of the mirror image. Your eye will be drawn to the middle of the hat, and above and below that point, the opposite design forms to create a gorgeous, dramatic effect. Plus, since this hat is knit with bulky yarn, it makes for a quick knit!

Construction

This hat is worked in the round seamlessly from the brim to the crown.

Size

One size. See the Finished Measurements section on the next page.

This hat features a folded brim, has some slouch and is designed for an adult head measuring up to 22" (55 cm). If you do not meet gauge in the stranded pattern (main body of the hat) with the suggested needles, change your needle size to meet gauge and ensure you achieve the right fit.

Materials

Yarn

Approximately 133 yds (122 m) total of bulky weight yarn in four contrasting colors

Color A: 87 yds (80 m)

Color B: 25 yds (23 m)

Color C: 12 yds (11 m)

Color D: 9 yds (9 m)

Shown In

Mitchell's Creations MRGO (100% superwash Merino wool) 109 yds (100 m) per 3.5 oz (100 g)

Color A: Love Me

Color B: BeLeaf

Color C: Marigold

Color D: Poppies

Recommended Yarn Substitutions

Malabrigo Yarn Chunky (100% Merino wool), 104 yds (95 m) per 3.5 oz (100 g)

Lion Brand Yarn Hue + Me (80% acrylic, 20% wool), 137 yds (125 m) per 4.4 oz (125 g)

Suggested Needles

US 10 (6 mm) 16" (40 cm) circular knitting needles, or size needed to meet gauge

US 11 (8 mm) 16" (40 cm) circular knitting needles, or size needed to meet gauge

US 11 (8 mm) double-pointed needles or US 11 (8 mm) circular knitting needles with a longer cord for Magic Loop method (page 165), or size needed to meet gauge

Notions

Scissors

Stitch marker

Tapestry needle

Finished Measurements

Circumference: 19.25" (48 cm)

Height (from the bottom of the folded brim): 10.25" (26 cm)

Gauge

14.5 sts x 19 rnds = 4" (10 cm) square in 1 x 1 ribbing (unstretched) using US 10 (6 mm) needles

12.5 sts x 17 rnds = 4" (10 cm) square in the stranded pattern (main body of the hat) using US 11 (8 mm) needles

Abbreviations

dpns = double-pointed needles

k = knit

k2tog = knit two together

p = purl

rnd(s) = round(s)

st(s) = stitch(es)

Tips to Help You Visualize Your Project and Get You Started

You might consider choosing your color combo by starting in the middle of the design with Color C. Then, choose a high contrast color for Color A, which surrounds Color C. From there, choose your Color D, which surrounds Color C and Color A. Last, pick your Color B and make sure it has a high contrast with Color D.

As a reminder, you can refer to the Colorwork Basics section (page 9) if you need help with any of the techniques used in this pattern.

PATTERN

Brim

Using US 10 (6 mm) circular knitting needles, cast on 60 sts using **Color A**. Place a stitch marker and join in the round.

Rnds 1–29 (**Color A**): *k1, p1; repeat from * to end.

Your brim should measure roughly 6" (15 cm) from the cast-on edge at this point, resulting in a 3" (8-cm) cuffed brim. If it does not, just keep repeating the 1 x 1 rib pattern until it does.

Body

Please read through all of the following notes before beginning the chart.

Switch to US 11 (8 mm) circular knitting needles and follow the chart, working rounds 30–52.

Each stitch shown in the chart is a knit stitch. Each section of 4 stitches is repeated 15 times per round.

As I worked through the chart, I carried up my yarn along the inside of my hat in some places. To carry up your yarn, you can wrap your working yarn counterclockwise once around your unused yarn at the beginning of the round and then continue to work the chart. Just make sure to keep your yarn nice and tidy as you wrap so it doesn't get tangled. In spots where there was too much space until I began working with a color again, I cut my yarn. I will indicate those spots on the chart for you if you choose to use the same method. As always, use whatever method works best for you, my friends!

There are a couple of spots where you will want to minimize the appearance of jogs in your **Color B** stripes as you work the bottom and top (see page 164 for more on jogs). This can be done simply by slipping the first stitch of the second round in those cases. This is also indicated on the chart.

And just as a heads up, in rounds 38 and 44 you will be working with three colors at a time. Make sure to maintain your yarn position for each of the three colors as you work. I pulled **Color D** from the top, **Color A** from the middle and **Color B** from the bottom since that was the order in which I worked with them.

Your hat should measure 8.5" (21 cm) from the bottom of your folded brim after finishing the chart. If it does not, or if you would prefer a bit more slouch, continue knitting in the round using **Color A** until you reach that measurement/your desired height before moving on to the **Crown** section. Any modification will affect the amount of yarn used.

Crown

Switch to dpns or Magic Loop method (page 165) when your stitches become too tight on your needles.

Use **Color A** for all remaining rounds.

Rnd 53: *k4, k2tog; repeat from * to end. [50 sts]

Rnd 54: k to end.

Rnd 55: *k3, k2tog; repeat from * to end. [40 sts]

Rnd 56: k to end.

Rnd 57: *k2, k2tog; repeat from * to end. [30 sts]

Rnd 58: k to end.

Rnd 59: *k1, k2tog; repeat from * to end. [20 sts]

Rnd 60: k to end.

Rnd 61: *k2tog; repeat from * to end. [10 sts]

Finishing

Cut **Color A**, making sure to leave a tail roughly 12" (30 cm) long. Thread the tail through a tapestry needle and then weave it through the live stitches to take your work off your needles. Pull the tail tightly to close the top of your hat.

Weave in all remaining ends.

Mirror Chart

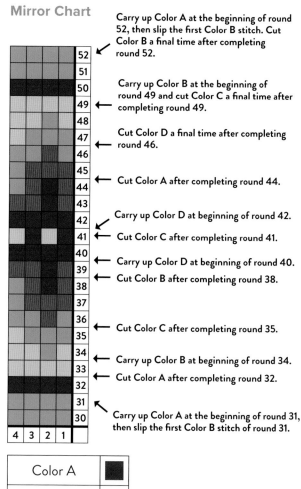

Carry up Color A at the beginning of round 52, then slip the first Color B stitch. Cut Color B a final time after completing round 52.

Carry up Color B at the beginning of round 49 and cut Color C a final time after completing round 49.

Cut Color D a final time after completing round 46.

Cut Color A after completing round 44.

Carry up Color D at beginning of round 42.

Cut Color C after completing round 41.

Carry up Color D at beginning of round 40.

Cut Color B after completing round 38.

Cut Color C after completing round 35.

Carry up Color B at beginning of round 34.

Cut Color A after completing round 32.

Carry up Color A at the beginning of round 31, then slip the first Color B stitch of round 31.

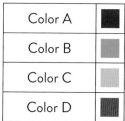

Color A	
Color B	
Color C	
Color D	

Give your work a gentle horizontal tug to stretch out those floats and help shape your hat. I highly recommend steam blocking this beauty to smooth out your stitches.

MYRIAD

I designed this hat to give you plenty of options to customize color combos and incorporate design elements in any way you like. If you're feeling adventurous, you could choose up to six colors. If you prefer a more subtle look, go for just two. Do you want to include the colorwork in each section or just one? It's totally up to you! So many choices! What will you pick?

Construction

This hat is worked in the round seamlessly from the brim to the crown.

Size

One size. See the Finished Measurements section on page 122.

This hat is designed for an adult head measuring up to 23" (58 cm). If you do not meet gauge in the stranded pattern (main body of the hat) with the suggested needles, change your needle size to meet gauge and ensure you achieve the right fit.

Materials

Yarn

Approximately 194 yds (178 m) total of worsted weight yarn in up to six contrasting colors

Color A: 51 yds (47 m)

Color B: 23 yds (21 m)

Color C: 23 yds (21 m)

Color D: 23 yds (21 m)

Color E: 51 yds (47 m)

Color F: 23 yds (21 m)

Shown In (hat with all three sections)

Neighborhood Fiber Co. Organic Studio Worsted (100% organic Merino wool), 200 yds (183 m) per 4 oz (114 g)

Color A: Penn North

Color B: Bolton Hill

Color C: Waverly

Neighborhood Fiber Co. Studio Worsted (100% superwash Merino wool), 200 yds (183 m) per 4 oz (114 g)

Color D: Federal Hill

Color E: Basquiat

Color F: Ramblewood

Recommended Yarn Substitution

Lion Brand Yarn Wool-Ease (80% acrylic, 20% wool), 197 yds (180 m) per 3 oz (85 g)

Suggested Needles

US 7 (4.5 mm) 16" (40 cm) circular knitting needles, or size needed to meet gauge

US 9 (5.5 mm) 16" (40 cm) circular knitting needles, or size needed to meet gauge

US 9 (5.5 mm) double-pointed needles or US 9 (5.5 mm) circular knitting needles with a longer cord for Magic Loop method (page 165), or size needed to meet gauge

Notions

4 stitch markers, 1 unique for beginning of round

Scissors

Tapestry needle

Finished Measurements

Circumference: 18.75" (47 cm)

Height: 9.25" (23 cm)

Gauge

20 sts = 4" (10 cm) and 9 rounds = 1.5" (4 cm) in 1 x 1 ribbing (unstretched) using US 7 (4.5 mm) needles

17 sts x 21 rnds = 4" (10 cm) square in the stranded and stockinette pattern (main body of the hat) using US 9 (5.5 mm) needles

Abbreviations

dpns = double-pointed needles

k = knit

k2tog = knit two together

p = purl

rnd(s) = round(s)

st(s) = stitch(es)

Tips to Help You Visualize Your Project and Get You Started

This is such a fun hat, my friends, with so many options to choose from to make it your own! I recommend just playing around with colors you have in your stash. If you have a little bit of everything, you might consider including the colorwork in all three sections of the pattern. If you don't have six colors on hand, you can choose to knit just the first section following the colorwork design and then knit the other two sections in stockinette using different colors or just one color. Or maybe you prefer the middle section to include the colorwork design. Then, you can choose to knit the section above and below it in stockinette—again, using a different color for each section or one color for both. This pattern is great for using whatever small amounts of worsted yarn you might have available!

Whatever works best for you, just make sure you choose yarn with a high contrast between colors within each section as well as between sections.

As a reminder, you can refer to the Colorwork Basics section (page 9) if you need help with any of the techniques used in this pattern.

PATTERN

Brim

Using US 7 (4.5 mm) circular knitting needles, cast on 80 sts using **Color A**. Place your unique stitch marker and join in the round.

Rnds 1–9 (**Color A**): *k1, p1; repeat from * to end.

Body

Switch to US 9 (5.5 mm) circular knitting needles.

Rnd 10 (**Color A**): *k20, place marker; repeat from * to end. The markers will help you better visualize the beginning and end of each repeat.

Please read through all of the following notes before beginning the chart.

Work chart rounds 11–44.

All stitches shown in the chart are knit stitches. Each section of 20 stitches is repeated 4 times per round.

I cut my colors after each section in which I used them except for **Color E**, which is used to complete the **Crown** section. Use whatever method works best for you!

To minimize the appearance of jogs in your work, slip the first **Color C** stitch of round 22 purl-wise and continue knitting the round as called for in the chart (see page 164 for more on jogs). You can also do this for **Color E** in round 33. These spots will be indicated for you on the chart.

Remove the markers placed in round 10 as you work round 42.

Myriad Chart

Your hat should measure about 8″ (20 cm) from the cast-on edge after finishing the chart. If it does not, or if you would prefer a bit more slouch, continue knitting in the round using **Color E** (or the color you used for round 44) until you reach that measurement/your desired length before moving on to the **Crown** section. Any modification will affect the amount of yarn used.

Crown

Switch to dpns or Magic Loop method when your stitches become too tight on your needles.

Use **Color E** for all remaining rounds.

Rnd 45: *k3, k2tog; repeat from * to end. [64 sts]

Rnd 46: k to end.

Rnd 47: *k2, k2tog; repeat from * to end. [48 sts]

Rnd 48: k to end.

Rnd 49: *k1, k2tog; repeat from * to end. [32 sts]

Rnd 50: k to end.

Rnd 51: *k2tog; repeat from * to end. [16 sts]

Finishing

Cut **Color E** (or the color you used to complete your hat), making sure to leave a tail about 12″ (30 cm) long. Thread the tail through a tapestry needle and then weave it through the live stitches to take your work off your needles. Pull the tail tightly to close the top of your hat. Weave in all remaining ends.

I recommend blocking this hat to smooth out that colorwork and fully showcase the design.

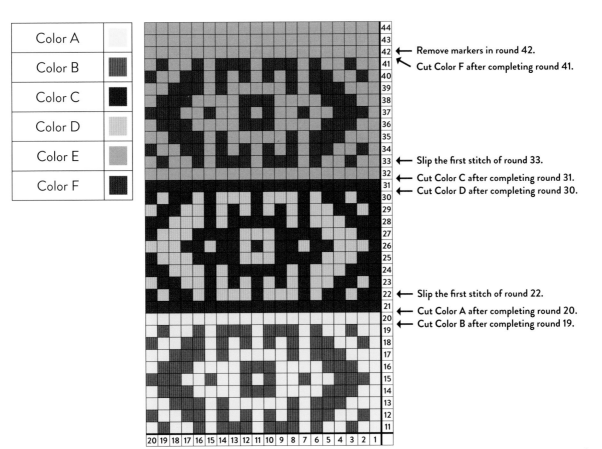

Color A	
Color B	
Color C	
Color D	
Color E	
Color F	

← Remove markers in round 42.
↖ Cut Color F after completing round 41.

← Slip the first stitch of round 33.
← Cut Color C after completing round 31.
← Cut Color D after completing round 30.

← Slip the first stitch of round 22.
← Cut Color A after completing round 20.
← Cut Color B after completing round 19.

GLOW

This design reminds me of little matches or candles popping up from the brim of the hat that are topped off by glowing squares and little "embers" that fade into the crown. Knit with worsted weight yarn, this baby is super versatile and lightweight enough to wear indoors or outside in chilly weather. And although I designed it as fitted hat, there are also simple modifications you can use to make it slouchy if you prefer!

Construction

This hat is worked in the round seamlessly from the brim to the crown.

Size

One size. See the Finished Measurements section below.

This fitted hat is designed for an adult head measuring up to 23" (58 cm). If you do not meet gauge in the stranded pattern (main body of the hat) with the suggested needles, change your needle size to meet gauge and ensure you achieve the right fit.

Finished Measurements

Circumference: 18.75" (47 cm)

Height: 8.75" (22 cm)

Gauge

18.5 sts = 4" (10 cm) and 9 rnds = 1.5" (4 cm) in 1 x 1 ribbing (unstretched) using US 7 (4.5 mm) needles

17 sts x 19 rnds = 4" (10 cm) square knit in the stranded pattern (main body of the hat) using US 9 (5.5 mm) needles

Materials

Yarn

Approximately 161 yds (148 m) total of worsted weight yarn in three contrasting colors

Color A: 97 yds (89 m)

Color B: 39 yds (36 m)

Color C: 25 yds (23 m)

Shown In

OMG Yarn (Balls) Liberty (100% superwash Merino wool), 220 yds (202 m) per 3.5 oz (100 g)

Color A: Serenity

Color B: Command

Color C: Sandshoes

Recommended Yarn Substitution

Lion Brand Yarn Wool-Ease (80% acrylic, 20% wool), 197 yds (180 m) per 3 oz (85 g)

Suggested Needles

US 7 (4.5 mm) 16" (40 cm) circular knitting needles, or size needed to meet gauge

US 9 (5.5 mm) 16" (40 cm) circular knitting needles, or size needed to meet gauge

US 9 (5.5 mm) double-pointed needles or US 9 (5.5 mm) circular knitting needles with a longer cord for Magic Loop method (page 165), or size needed to meet gauge

Notions

Scissors

Stitch marker

Tapestry needle

Abbreviations

dpns = double-pointed needles

k = knit

k2tog = knit two together

p = purl

rnd(s) = round(s)

st(s) = stitch(es)

Tips to Help You Visualize Your Project and Get You Started

I just love how the colors seem to radiate in this design, my friends. Starting with the corrugated brim, the colors continue to "burn" throughout the rest of the pattern. You can choose to go with a fade of colors—think red, orange and yellow or even green, blue and purple—or you can pick colors with a stark contrast like I did and use a deep purple, red and light beige for a bold look. There are so many possibilities! Just choose your favorites and dive into that stash.

As a reminder, you can refer to the Colorwork Basics section (page 9) if you need help with any of the techniques used in this pattern.

PATTERN

Brim

Using US 7 (4.5 mm) circular knitting needles, cast on 80 sts using **Color A**. Place a stitch marker and join in the round.

Rnds 1–9: *k1 (**Color B**), p1 (**Color A**); repeat from * to end.

Body

Please read through all of the following notes before beginning the chart.

Switch to US 9 (5.5 mm) circular knitting needles and follow the chart, working rounds 10–32.

All stitches shown in the chart are knit stitches. Each section of 8 stitches is repeated 10 times per round.

As you knit the hat, there will be a few spots where you will want to carry up your yarn when it is not being used. At the beginning of rounds 17 and 26 you will want to carry up **Color C**. You can do this by wrapping **Color A** (your working yarn) counter-clockwise once around **Color C** (your unused yarn) and then continuing to work the chart. I will indicate these spots on the chart as a friendly reminder!

And just as a heads up, you will be working with three colors at a time in rounds 19–23. Make sure to maintain your yarn position for each of the three colors as you work. I pulled **Color C** from the top, **Color B** from the middle and **Color A** from the bottom since that was the order in which I worked with them.

Also, as you knit the hat, there will be a few spots where you will want to catch floats as they tend to be too long otherwise. You can do this by floating the unused color, making sure to leave plenty of slack. Then, on the next round, when you reach the middle of the long float, pick it up with your left needle and knit it together with the next stitch. These spots also will be indicated on the chart.

I cut **Color B** after rounds 13, 23 and a final time after round 32. I cut **Color C** after round 28.

Glow Chart

Your hat should measure about 6.25" (16 cm) from the cast-on edge after completing the chart.

Once you complete the chart, continue knitting in the round with **Color A** until your hat reaches 7.5" (19 cm) from the cast-on edge before moving on to the **Crown** section.

If you prefer a hat with more slouch, you can continue knitting in the round with **Color A** to your desired height before moving on to the **Crown** section. Any modifications will affect the amount of yarn used.

Crown

Switch to dpns or Magic Loop method (page 165) when your stitches become too tight on your needles.

Use **Color A** for all remaining rounds.

Rnd 1: *k3, k2tog; repeat from * to end. [64 sts]

Rnd 2: k to end.

Rnd 3: *k2, k2tog; repeat from * to end. [48 sts]

Rnd 4: k to end.

Rnd 5: *k1, k2tog; repeat from * to end. [32 sts]

Rnd 6: k to end.

Rnd 7: *k2tog; repeat from * to end. [16 sts]

Finishing

Cut **Color A**, making sure to leave a tail about 12" (30 cm) long. Thread the tail through a tapestry needle and then weave it through the live stitches to take your work off your needles. Pull the tail tightly to close the top of your hat.

Weave in all remaining ends.

I recommend steam blocking this hat to smooth out your floats and help shape it.

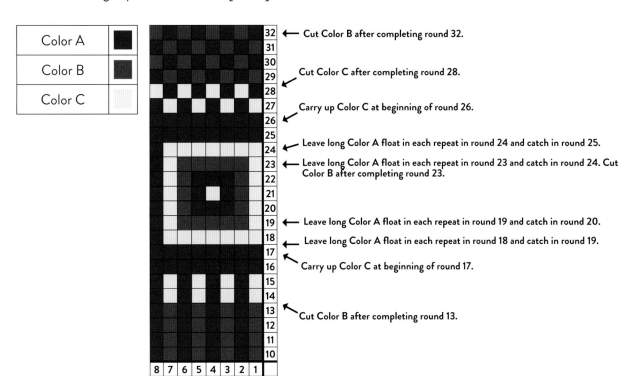

Color A	■
Color B	■
Color C	▦

← Cut Color B after completing round 32.

← Cut Color C after completing round 28.

← Carry up Color C at beginning of round 26.

← Leave long Color A float in each repeat in round 24 and catch in round 25.

← Leave long Color A float in each repeat in round 23 and catch in round 24. Cut Color B after completing round 23.

← Leave long Color A float in each repeat in round 19 and catch in round 20.

← Leave long Color A float in each repeat in round 18 and catch in round 19.

← Carry up Color C at beginning of round 17.

← Cut Color B after completing round 13.

LEVEL UP

I designed this hat to be super customizable with a range of color combos depending on what yarn you have on hand. Just choose two or more colors and get to work on each "level" of your hat. The middle color of each diamond shape becomes the outer part of the shape as you level up, making it so much fun to see the design build as you knit. This pattern is written for child and adult sizes, and you can even make this baby slouchy or more fitted.

Construction

This hat is worked in the round seamlessly from the brim to the crown.

Size

Measurements and information pertaining to child and adult sizes will be noted throughout this pattern as follows: Child (Adult). See the Finished Measurements section on page 130.

This hat is designed for the average Child (Adult) head measuring up to 21 (23)"/53 (58) cm. If you do not meet gauge in the stranded pattern (main body of the hat) with the suggested needles, change your needle size to meet gauge and ensure you achieve the right fit. The sizing also can be adjusted by reducing or adding cast-on stitches in multiples of 4. Any modification will affect the amount of yarn used.

Materials

Yarn

Approximately 123 (156) yds/113 (143) m total of Aran or heavy worsted weight yarn in at least two contrasting colors

Color A: 75 (81) yds/69 (75) m

Color B: 12 (15) yds/11 (14) m

Color C: 12 (15) yds/11 (14) m

Color D: 12 (15) yds/11 (14) m

Color E: 12 (15) yds/11 (14) m

Color F: 12 (15) yds/11 (14) m

Please note that you do not need **Color F** for the Child hat.

Shown In

Fully Spun Postscript Aran (100% superwash Merino wool), 177 yds (162 m) per 3.5 oz (100 g)

Color A: In the North

Color B: Loyal Pup

Color C: Killer Eggplant

Color D: Good Navy

Color E: August 6th

Color F: Loyal Pup

Recommended Yarn Substitution

Big Twist Classic (100% acrylic), 690 yds (630 m) per 11 oz (310 g)

Suggested Needles

US 8 (5 mm) 16" (40 cm) circular knitting needles, or size needed to meet gauge

US 10 (6 mm) 16" (40 cm) circular knitting needles, or size needed to meet gauge

US 10 (6 mm) double-pointed needles or US 10 (6 mm) circular knitting needles with a longer cord for Magic Loop method (page 165), or size needed to meet gauge

Notions

Scissors

Stitch marker

Tapestry needle

Finished Measurements

Circumference: 17 (18.75)"/43 (47) cm

Height: 8 (9.25)"/20 (23) cm

Gauge

19 sts = 4" (10 cm) and 9 rnds = 1.5" (4 cm) in 1 x 1 twisted ribbing (unstretched) using US 8 (5 mm) needles

17 sts x 19 rnds = 4" (10 cm) square in the stranded pattern (main body of the hat) using US 10 (6 mm) needles

Abbreviations

dpns = double-pointed needles

k = knit

k1tbl = knit one stitch through the back loop

k2tog = knit two together

p = purl

rnd(s) = round(s)

st(s) = stitch(es)

Tips to Help You Visualize Your Project and Get You Started

*There are so many color combos you can choose for this hat! I recommend picking your background color (**Color A**) first and then choosing the colors you want to use for each "level." You can go with a black background and pick a rainbow of neon hues for the levels. Or you can keep it simple and pick a background color and just one contrasting color so each level is the same. It's totally up to you!*

As a reminder, you can refer to the Colorwork Basics section (page 9) if you need help with any of the techniques used in this pattern.

PATTERN

Brim

Using US 8 (5 mm) circular knitting needles, cast on 72 (80) sts using **Color A**. Place your stitch marker and join in the round.

Rnds 1–9 (**Color A**): *k1tbl, p1; repeat from * to end.

Body

Please read through all of the following notes before beginning the chart.

Switch to US 10 (6 mm) circular knitting needles and work chart as indicated for your size:

Child: Work rounds 10–33 once, then knit 1 round in **Color A**.

Adult: Work rounds 10–40 (see below for modifications).

Each stitch shown in the chart is a knit stitch. Each section of 4 stitches shown in the chart is repeated 19 (20) times per round.

There will be some spots in the chart where you will want to minimize the appearance of jogs in diamonds that span across the join (see page 164 for more on jogs). You can do this by knitting the final stitch of rounds 12 and 13, 18 and 19, 24 and 25, 30 and 31 and 36 and 37 (for the adult version) in the reverse color. I will indicate these spots on the chart to help you out!

I cut my colors after I was done using them in each section, but use whatever method works best for you. Do not cut **Color A**, as you use it throughout.

Level Up Chart

Your hat should measure roughly 6.5 (8.25)"/ 16 (21) cm from the cast-on edge after you complete the chart.

If you are knitting the adult version and prefer a hat that is shorter, you can complete round 33, knit one round in **Color A** and then move on to the **Crown** section. If you prefer a slouchier hat, you can repeat rounds 34–39 once or twice more in your desired color to add extra "levels," knit one round in **Color A** and then move on to the **Crown** section. Any modifications will affect the amount of yarn used.

Crown

Switch to dpns or Magic Loop method (page 165) when your stitches become too tight on your needles.

Use **Color A** for all remaining rounds.

If you modified your cast-on to a number that results in an odd number when divided by 4, you can knit the last stitch of round 41 (47).

Rnd 35 (41): *k2, k2tog; repeat from * to end. [54 (60) sts]

Rnd 36 (42): k to end.

Rnd 37 (43): *k1, k2tog; repeat from * to end. [36 (40) sts]

Rnd 38 (44): k to end.

Rnd 39 (45): *k2tog; repeat from * to end. [18 (20) sts]

Rnd 40 (46): k to end.

Rnd 41 (47): *k2tog; repeat from * to end. [9 (10) sts]

Finishing

Cut **Color A**, making sure to leave a tail roughly 12" (30 cm) long. Thread the tail through a tapestry needle and then weave it through the live stitches to take your work off your needles. Pull the tail tightly to close the top of your hat.

Weave in all remaining ends.

Give your work a gentle horizontal tug to stretch out those floats and help shape your hat. I highly recommend steam blocking this hat to smooth out all your levels.

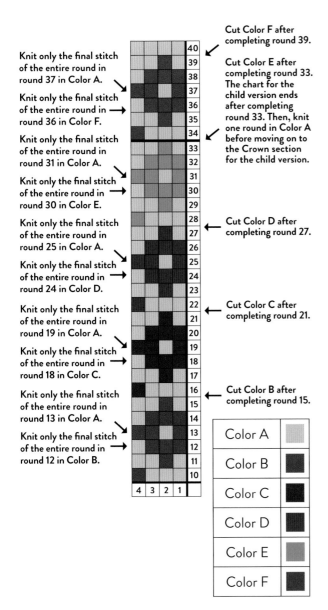

Knit only the final stitch of the entire round in round 37 in Color A.

Knit only the final stitch of the entire round in round 36 in Color F.

Knit only the final stitch of the entire round in round 31 in Color A.

Knit only the final stitch of the entire round in round 30 in Color E.

Knit only the final stitch of the entire round in round 25 in Color A.

Knit only the final stitch of the entire round in round 24 in Color D.

Knit only the final stitch of the entire round in round 19 in Color A.

Knit only the final stitch of the entire round in round 18 in Color C.

Knit only the final stitch of the entire round in round 13 in Color A.

Knit only the final stitch of the entire round in round 12 in Color B.

Cut Color F after completing round 39.

Cut Color E after completing round 33. The chart for the child version ends after completing round 33. Then, knit one round in Color A before moving on to the Crown section for the child version.

Cut Color D after completing round 27.

Cut Color C after completing round 21.

Cut Color B after completing round 15.

Color A	
Color B	
Color C	
Color D	
Color E	
Color F	

I know we all love hats here, and what better time of year to showcase those cozy accessories in all their glory than in the fall and winter seasons?

This chapter is filled with patterns featuring whimsical, bold designs that show the world just how much you love hat weather! From September through February and beyond, you'll find so many options in these pages to keep you toasty.

In Nuts about Autumn (page 135), you'll find a cozy, folded brim and a series of acorns that form around the body of the hat. If you're looking for all the spooky vibes, Eek-A-Boo! (page 145) has you covered with a playful design that mixes the words "Eek" and "Boo" with little skull shapes—so delightfully scary! And you'll find all the love wrapped up in Queen of Hearts (page 159), an awesome pattern to knit up for Valentine's Day, or really any day you want to feel like a queen.

So let's celebrate! Celebrate the magic of the season you're in or the one you're heading into by picking the perfect design for the occasion from these pages. Celebrate the artist within you as you choose the color combinations you'll use to make these patterns. And always celebrate your creations as your own masterpieces that you made with the power of your imagination and your own two hands.

Cheers to all of you, my friends!

NUTS ABOUT AUTUMN

I have a major obsession with acorns, and I designed this hat to showcase their awesomeness. They're like little woodland snowflakes—each one is unique from color to cap. And when they start to fall from oak trees, well, you just know it's a total sign that autumn has arrived. And I definitely love fall most of all! Who's with me?

Construction

This hat is worked in the round seamlessly from the brim to the crown.

Size

One size. See the Finished Measurements section on the next page.

This hat is designed for an adult head measuring up to 23" (58 cm). If you do not meet gauge in the stranded pattern (main body of the hat) with the suggested needles, change your needle size to meet gauge and ensure you achieve the right fit.

Materials

Yarn

Approximately 200 yds (183 m) total of worsted weight yarn in four contrasting colors

Color A: 96 yds (88 m)

Color B: 30 yds (28 m)

Color C: 33 yds (31 m)

Color D: 41 yds (38 m)

Shown In

Neighborhood Fiber Co. Studio Worsted (100% superwash Merino wool), 200 yds (183 m) per 4 oz (114 g)

Color A: Cooper Circle

Color B: Federal Hill

Color C: Ramblewood

Color D: Oaklee

Recommended Yarn Substitution

Lion Brand Yarn Wool-Ease (80% acrylic, 20% wool), 197 yds (180 m) per 3 oz (85 g)

Suggested Needles

US 7 (4.5 mm) 16" (40 cm) circular knitting needles, or size needed to meet gauge

US 9 (5.5 mm) 16" (40 cm) circular knitting needles, or size needed to meet gauge

US 9 (5.5 mm) double-pointed needles or US 9 (5.5 mm) circular knitting needles with a longer cord for Magic Loop method (page 165), or size needed to meet gauge

Notions

Scissors

Stitch marker

Tapestry needle

Finished Measurements

Circumference: 20" (50 cm)

Height (from the bottom of the folded brim): 9.5" (24 cm)

Gauge

18.5 sts x 25 rnds = 4" (10 cm) square in 1 x 1 ribbing (unstretched) using US 7 (4.5 mm) needles

17 sts x 20 rnds = 4" (10 cm) square in the stranded pattern (main body of the hat) using US 9 (5.5 mm) needles

Abbreviations

dpns = double-pointed needles

k = knit

k2tog = knit two together

p = purl

rnd(s) = round(s)

st(s) = stitch(es)

Tips to Help You Visualize Your Project and Get You Started

*Acorns are awesome, and they tend to range in color from deep browns to silver grays. You might start by choosing the two colors you want to use for your acorns (**Color B** and **Color C**) and then pick your other two colors from there. If you love the fall vibe as much as I do, you might consider yellows, oranges or reds for your secondary colors. Just make sure the color surrounding your acorns (**Color D**) has a high contrast against them. I used tonal yarn for **Color A** and **Color D**, and I love the dimension it adds to the finished piece.*

As a reminder, you can refer to the Colorwork Basics section (page 9) if you need help with any of the techniques used in this pattern.

PATTERN

Brim

Using US 7 (4.5 mm) circular knitting needles, cast on 84 sts using **Color A**. Place a stitch marker and join in the round.

Rnds 1–35 (**Color A**): *k1, p1; repeat from * to end.

Your brim should measure roughly 5.5" (14 cm) from the cast-on edge at this point, resulting in a 2.75" (7-cm) folded brim. If it does not, just keep repeating the 1 x 1 rib pattern until it does.

Rnd 36 (**Color A**): k to end.

Cut **Color A**.

Body

Please read through all of the following notes before beginning the chart.

Switch to US 9 (5.5 mm) circular knitting needles and follow the chart, working rounds 37–61.

All stitches shown in the chart are knit stitches. Each section of 6 stitches is repeated 14 times per round.

I cut my colors after each section in which I used them. Use whatever method works best for you!

At the beginning of round 52, you will want to carry up **Color C**. You can do this by wrapping **Color D** (your working yarn) counterclockwise once around **Color C** (your unused yarn) and then continuing to work the chart. This will be indicated on the chart to help you out.

Cut **Color B** and **Color C** after you complete round 57.

To minimize the appearance of a jog in your work, slip the first **Color D** stitch of round 59 purl-wise and continue knitting the round as called for in the chart. This also will be indicated for you on the chart.

Nuts about Autumn Chart

Your hat should measure about 7.75" (19 cm) from the bottom of your folded brim after finishing the chart. If it does not, or if you would prefer a bit more slouch, continue knitting in the round using **Color D** until you reach that measurement/your desired height before moving on to the **Crown** section. Any modification will affect the amount of yarn used.

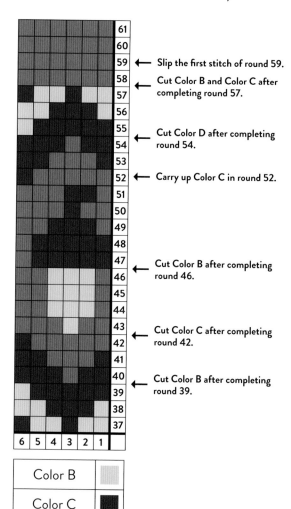

61
60
59 ← Slip the first stitch of round 59.
58 ← Cut Color B and Color C after
57   completing round 57.
56
55 ← Cut Color D after completing
54   round 54.
53
52 ← Carry up Color C in round 52.
51
50
49
48
47 ← Cut Color B after completing
46   round 46.
45
44
43 ← Cut Color C after completing
42   round 42.
41
40 ← Cut Color B after completing
39   round 39.
38
37

6 5 4 3 2 1

Color B	
Color C	
Color D	

Crown

Switch to dpns or Magic Loop method (page 165) when your stitches become too tight on your needles.

Use **Color D** for all remaining rounds.

Rnd 62: *k4, k2tog; repeat from * to end. [70 sts]

Rnd 63: k to end.

Rnd 64: *k3, k2tog; repeat from * to end. [56 sts]

Rnd 65: k to end.

Rnd 66: *k2, k2tog; repeat from * to end. [42 sts]

Rnd 67: k to end.

Rnd 68: *k1, k2tog; repeat from * to end. [28 sts]

Rnd 69: k to end.

Rnd 70: *k2tog; repeat from * to end. [14 sts]

Finishing

Cut **Color D**, making sure to leave a tail about 12" (30 cm) long. Thread the tail through a tapestry needle and then weave it through the live stitches to take your work off your needles. Pull the tail tightly to close the top of your hat.

Weave in all remaining ends.

I recommend blocking this hat to smooth out those acorns and showcase them in all their glory.

FALL FEELS

I designed this hat to give you all the fall feels! You can choose to knit little apples or pumpkins, making this a perfect go-to hat for autumn whether you're picking apples at the orchard or pumpkins at the patch. The apple design also makes a great gift for that special teacher in your life. And if you're making the pumpkin version, there are options to make taller pumpkins or shorter versions that look more like gourds. So many fun possibilities to celebrate the season!

Construction

This hat is worked in the round seamlessly from the brim to the crown.

Size

One size. See the Finished Measurements section below.

This is a fitted hat designed for an adult head measuring up to 22" (55 cm). If you do not meet gauge in the stranded pattern (main body of the hat) with the suggested needles, change your needle size to meet gauge and ensure you achieve the right fit.

Finished Measurements

Circumference: 18.25" (46 cm)

Height: 9" (23 cm)

Gauge

16 sts = 4" (10 cm) and 7 rnds = 1.5" (4 cm) in 1 x 1 twisted ribbing (unstretched) using US 9 (5.5 mm) needles

14 sts x 17 rnds = 4" (10 cm) square in the stranded pattern (main body of the hat) using US 10.5 (6.5 mm) needles

Materials

Yarn

Approximately 114 yds (105 m) total of bulky weight yarn in four contrasting colors

Color A: 49 yds (45 m)

Color B: 36 yds (33 m)

Color C: 26 yds (24 m)

Color D: 3 yds (3 m)

Shown In

Malabrigo Yarn Chunky (100% Merino wool), 104 yds (95 m) per 3.5 oz (100 g)

Color A: Rhodesian Ridgeback (pumpkin), Ravelry Red (apple)

Color B: Marron Oscuro

Color C: Natural

Color D: Lettuce

Recommended Yarn Substitution

Loops & Threads Charisma™ (100% acrylic), 109 yds (100 m) per 3.5 oz (100 g)

Suggested Needles

US 9 (5.5 mm) 16" (40 cm) circular knitting needles, or size needed to meet gauge

US 10.5 (6.5 mm) 16" (40 cm) circular knitting needles, or size needed to meet gauge

US 10.5 (6.5 mm) double-pointed needles or US 10.5 (6.5 mm) circular knitting needles with a longer cord for Magic Loop method (page 165), or size needed to meet gauge

Notions

Scissors

Stitch marker

Tapestry needle

Abbreviations

dpns = double-pointed needles

k = knit

k1tbl = knit one stitch through the back loop

k2tog = knit two together

p = purl

rnd(s) = round(s)

st(s) = stitch(es)

Tips to Help You Visualize Your Project and Get You Started

*The first thing you'll need to decide is whether you want to knit apples or pumpkins, which will determine whether **Color A**, and therefore your hat, has more of a red or orange vibe (if you choose to go with traditional apple/pumpkin colors). From there, I recommend choosing a **Color C** (background color) with high contrast, so the apples or pumpkins really pop. The wavy pattern near the brim and the stripes of the crown then will be a mixture of the colors you choose for **Color A** and **Color B**. So much fall goodness wrapped up in this one, my friends! Have fun knitting this baby up and wearing it in the crisp, autumn air.*

As a reminder, you can refer to the Colorwork Basics section (page 9) if you need help with any of the techniques used in this pattern.

PATTERN

Brim

Using US 9 (5.5 mm) circular knitting needles, cast on 64 sts using **Color A**. Place a stitch marker and join in the round.

Rnds 1–7 (**Color A**): *k1tbl, p1; repeat from * to end.

Body

Please read through all of the following notes before beginning the chart.

Switch to US 10.5 (6.5 mm) circular knitting needles and follow the chart, working rounds 8–33.

Each stitch shown in the chart is a knit stitch. Each section of 8 stitches shown in the chart is repeated 8 times per round.

I cut my colors after some sections and carried up my yarn in others. At the beginning of round 21, I carried up **Color B** so I could use it in the striped section near the crown. You can do this by wrapping **Color C** (your working yarn) counterclockwise once around **Color B** (your unused yarn) and then continuing to work the chart. I cut **Color A** after completing rounds 10, 18 and 30. I cut **Color B** after completing round 13. I cut **Color D** after completing round 20. I cut **Color C** after completing round 22. I will indicate all these spots on the chart as a friendly reminder if you choose to do what I did! As always, feel free to use whatever method works best for you!

In round 19, you will have long **Color B** floats, and in round 20 you will have long **Color B** and **Color D** floats. I recommend catching those floats. You can do this by floating the unused color(s), making sure to leave plenty of slack. Then, on the next round, when you reach the middle of the long float, pick it up with your left needle and knit it together with the next stitch. This will be indicated on the chart to help you out!

If you prefer a shorter pumpkin that looks more like a gourd, you can omit round 17 and continue to work the chart, repeating round 33 once more to maintain the overall height of the hat. If you'd like to knit a taller pumpkin, you can repeat round 17 twice more and then continue to work the chart, omitting rounds 29 and 30 to maintain the overall height of the hat. (I repeated round 17 twice more and omitted rounds 29 and 30 for the sample pumpkin hat I knit. I knit my sample apple hat according to the chart.)

Your pumpkins or apples may appear a little scrunched as you knit because you are carrying longer floats to create them that haven't been stretched. Don't panic, my friends! Just make sure to keep those floats nice and loose, and the shapes should smooth out nicely when you block it after you finish your hat.

Also, just as a heads up, in rounds 19 and 20 you will be working with three colors at a time. Make sure to maintain your yarn position for each of the three colors as you work. I pulled **Color C** from the top, **Color B** from the middle and **Color D** from the bottom since that was the order in which I worked with them.

You also may want to minimize the appearance of jogs in your stripes toward the top of the hat by following these steps (see page 164 for more on jogs):

Knit your first round of stripes using **Color B** as called for in the chart. Once you reach the end of the round, remove your stitch marker. Insert your right needle purl-wise into the right leg of the **Color C** stitch below the first **Color B** stitch on your left needle. Then, using your right needle, move that **Color C** stitch up onto your left needle so it is next to the **Color B** stitch. Knit those two stitches together. Replace your stitch marker. This will shift the beginning of your round to the left by one stitch and that is totally okay! (In subsequent rounds, **Color C** will be replaced by **Color A** as you work through the stripes.)

Knit your next round of stripes in **Color A** as called for in the chart. Once you reach the end of the round, remove your stitch marker. Insert your right needle purl-wise into the right leg of the **Color B** stitch below the first **Color A** stitch on your left needle. Then, using your right needle, move that **Color B** stitch up onto your left needle so it is next to the **Color A** stitch. Knit those two stitches together. Replace your stitch marker. Again, the beginning of your round will shift to the left by one stitch, and this is okay!

Repeat both steps as you work through the stripes on the crown.

Fall Feels Chart

Your hat should measure roughly 7.5" (19 cm) from the cast-on edge after you finish working the chart. If it does not or if you prefer a slouchier hat, you can continue knitting in the round using **Color B** to reach that measurement/your desired height before you move on to the **Crown** section. Any modification will affect the amount of yarn used.

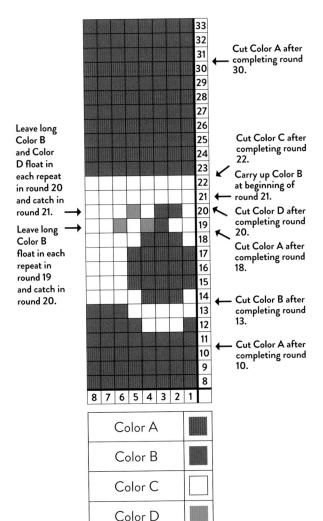

Leave long Color B and Color D float in each repeat in round 20 and catch in round 21. →

Leave long Color B float in each repeat in round 19 and catch in round 20. →

Cut Color A after completing round 30.

Cut Color C after completing round 22.

Carry up Color B at beginning of round 21.

Cut Color D after completing round 20.

Cut Color A after completing round 18.

Cut Color B after completing round 13.

Cut Color A after completing round 10.

Color A	■
Color B	■
Color C	□
Color D	■

Crown

Switch to dpns or Magic Loop method (page 165) when your stitches become too tight on your needles.

Use **Color B** for all remaining rounds.

Rnd 34: *k2, k2tog; repeat from * to end. [48 sts]

Rnd 35: k to end.

Rnd 36: *k1, k2tog; repeat from * to end. [32 sts]

Rnd 37: k to end.

Rnd 38: *k2tog; repeat from * to end. [16 sts]

Rnd 39: k to end.

Rnd 40: *k2tog; repeat from * to end. [8 sts]

Finishing

Cut **Color B**, making sure to leave a tail roughly 12" (30 cm) long. Thread the tail through a tapestry needle and then weave it through the live stitches to take your work off your needles. Pull the tail tightly to close the top of your hat.

Weave in all remaining ends.

Give your work a gentle horizontal tug to stretch out those floats and help shape your hat. I highly recommend steam blocking it to smooth out those gorgeous pumpkins and apples.

EEK-A-BOO!

This hat just screams Halloween! A mix of spooky words and skulls play across the body to create such a fun visual effect. This hat would make the perfect accessory for trick-or-treating with your kids or heading out to a Halloween party on a crisp, fall night. Boo!

Construction

This hat is worked in the round seamlessly from the brim to the crown.

Size

One size. See the Finished Measurements section below.

This is a fitted hat designed for an adult head measuring up to 23" (58 cm). If you do not meet gauge in the stranded pattern (main body of the hat) with the suggested needles, change your needle size to meet gauge and ensure you achieve the right fit.

Finished Measurements

Circumference: 19" (48 cm)

Height: 8.5" (21 cm)

Gauge

18 sts = 4" (10 cm) and 9 rounds = 1.5" (4 cm) in 1 x 1 twisted ribbing (unstretched) using US 8 (5 mm) needles

17 sts x 19 rnds = 4" (10 cm) square in the stranded pattern (main body of the hat) using US 10 (6 mm) needles

Materials

Yarn

Approximately 128 yds (118 m) total of Aran or heavy worsted weight yarn in two contrasting colors

Color A: 97 yds (89 m)

Color B: 31 yds (29 m)

Shown In

Fully Spun Postscript Aran (100% superwash Merino wool), 177 yds (162 m) per 3.5 oz (100 g)

Color A: Loyal Pup

Color B: Community Lesbian Pride

Recommended Yarn Substitution

Loops & Threads Impeccable (100% acrylic), 285 yds (260 m) per 4.5 oz (128 g)

Suggested Needles

US 8 (5 mm) 16" (40 cm) circular knitting needles, or size needed to meet gauge

US 10 (6 mm) 16" (40 cm) circular knitting needles, or size needed to meet gauge

US 10 (6 mm) double-pointed needles or US 10 (6 mm) circular knitting needles with a longer cord for Magic Loop method (page 165), or size needed to meet gauge

Notions

5 stitch markers, 1 unique for beginning of round

Scissors

Tapestry needle

Abbreviations

dpns = double-pointed needles

k = knit

k1tbl = knit one stitch through the back loop

k2tog = knit two together

p = purl

rnd(s) = round(s)

st(s) = stitch(es)

Tips to Help You Visualize Your Project and Get You Started

*I chose to go with traditional Halloween colors for the hat I made using black for **Color A** and a variegated yarn with hints of orange, white and purple tones for **Color B**. You could do the same by choosing to use one colorway each for **Color A** and **Color B**. Or you could create a scrappy version by using one colorway for **Color A** and then substituting in three separate colorways for **Color B** in each section of the hat. For example, you could knit the BOO! section in purple, the skulls in white and the EEK! section in orange. I recommend picking your background color (**Color A**) first and going from there!*

As a reminder, you can refer to the Colorwork Basics section (page 9) if you need help with any of the techniques used in this pattern.

PATTERN

Brim

Using US 8 (5 mm) circular knitting needles, cast on 80 sts using **Color A**. Place your unique stitch marker and join in the round.

Rnds 1–9 (**Color A**): *k1tbl, p1; repeat from * to end.

Body

Switch to US 10 (6 mm) circular knitting needles.

Rnd 10 (**Color A**): *k16, place marker; repeat from * to end. The markers will help you better visualize the beginning and end of each repeat.

Please read through all of the following notes before beginning the chart.

Work chart rounds 11–35.

Each stitch shown in the chart is a knit stitch. Each section of 16 stitches shown in the chart is repeated 5 times per round.

There will be two spots in the chart where you will want to minimize the appearance of a jog in a skull that spans across the join. You can do this by knitting the final stitch of rounds 19 and 22 in the reverse color. I will indicate these spots on the chart to help you out!

At the beginning of rounds 17 and 25, you will want to carry up **Color B**. You can do this simply by wrapping **Color A** (your working yarn) counterclockwise once around **Color B** (your unused yarn) and then continuing to work the chart. I will indicate both these spots on the chart as a friendly reminder!

Cut **Color B** after completing round 30.

Remove markers placed in round 10 as you work round 31.

Eek-A-Boo! Chart

Your hat should measure roughly 7" (18 cm) from the cast-on edge after you complete the chart. If it does not or if you prefer a slouchier hat, continue knitting in the round using **Color A** until you reach that measurement/your desired height before moving on to the **Crown** section. Any modification will affect the amount of yarn used.

Crown

Switch to dpns or Magic Loop method (page 165) when your stitches become too tight on your needles.

Use **Color A** for all remaining rounds.

Rnd 36: *k3, k2tog; repeat from * to end. [64 sts]

Rnd 37: k to end.

Rnd 38: *k2, k2tog; repeat from * to end. [48 sts]

Rnd 39: k to end.

Rnd 40: *k1, k2tog; repeat from * to end. [32 sts]

Rnd 41: k to end.

Rnd 42: *k2tog; repeat from * to end. [16 sts]

Finishing

Cut **Color A**, making sure to leave a tail roughly 12" (30 cm) long. Thread the tail through a tapestry needle and then weave it through the live stitches to take your work off your needles. Pull the tail tightly to close the top of your hat.

Weave in all remaining ends.

Give your work a gentle horizontal tug to stretch out those floats and help shape your hat. I highly recommend steam blocking this hat to smooth out the words and skulls.

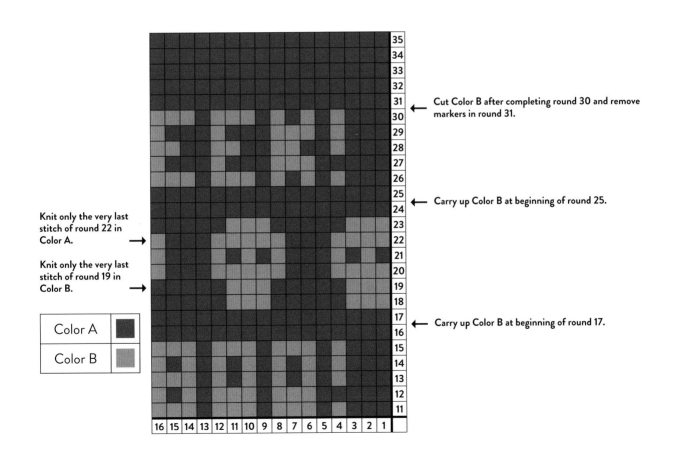

Cut Color B after completing round 30 and remove markers in round 31.

Carry up Color B at beginning of round 25.

Knit only the very last stitch of round 22 in Color A.

Knit only the very last stitch of round 19 in Color B.

Carry up Color B at beginning of round 17.

Color A

Color B

SNOWFALL

I designed this hat to look like snow falling gently from the sky and forming little piles toward the brim. There is a peaceful space that is created after the ground is blanketed with snow, and that's the feeling I want you to have when you wear this hat. You can also choose whether to make a fitted or slouchy version depending on your preference. And there's definitely no wrong answer! You might not even be able to resist making both.

Construction

This hat is worked in the round seamlessly from the brim to the crown.

Size

Measurements and other information pertaining to fitted and slouchy versions will be noted throughout this pattern as follows: Fitted (Slouchy). See the Finished Measurements section on page 149.

This hat is designed for an adult head measuring up to 22" (55 cm). If you do not meet gauge in the stranded pattern (main body of the hat) with the suggested needles, change your needle size to meet gauge and ensure you achieve the right fit.

Materials

Yarn

Approximately 97 (127) yds/89 (117) m total of bulky weight yarn in two contrasting colors

Color A: 40 (42) yds/37 (39) m

Color B: 57 (85) yds/53 (78) m

Shown In

Fitted version: Mountain Laurel Fiber Co. Chunky Singles (80% superwash Merino wool, 20% nylon), 76 yds (70 m) per 3.5 oz (100 g)

Color A: Vanilla Ice, Ice Baby

Color B: Tide Pools

Slouchy version: Malabrigo Yarn Mecha (100% superwash Merino wool), 130 yds (119 m) per 3.5 oz (100 g)

Color A: Natural

Color B: Azul Fresco

Recommended Yarn Substitutions

Fitted version: Lion Brand Yarn Hue + Me (80% acrylic, 20% wool), 137 yds (125 m) per 4.4 oz (125 g)

Slouchy version: Big Twist Classic (100% acrylic), 690 yds (630 m) per 11 oz (310 g)

Suggested Needles

US 9 (5.5 mm) 16" (40 cm) circular knitting needles, or size needed to meet gauge

US 10.5 (6.5 mm) 16" (40 cm) circular knitting needles, or size needed to meet gauge

US 10.5 (6.5 mm) double-pointed needles or US 10.5 (6.5 mm) circular knitting needles with a longer cord for Magic Loop method (page 165), or size needed to meet gauge

Notions

Scissors

Stitch marker

Tapestry needle

Finished Measurements

Fitted (Slouchy)

Circumference: 18.5 (18.5)"/46 (46 cm)

Height: 9.25 (10.5)"/23 (26) cm

Gauge

Fitted version: 13 sts = 4" (10 cm) and 9 rnds = 1.75" (4 cm) in 1 x 1 ribbing (unstretched) using US 9 (5.5 mm) needles

13 sts x 17 rnds = 4" (10 cm) square in the stranded pattern (main body of the hat) using US 10.5 (6.5 mm) needles

Slouchy version: 17 sts = 4" (10 cm) and 9 rounds = 1.5" (4 cm) in 1 x 1 ribbing (unstretched) using US 9 (5.5 mm) needles

15.5 sts x 21 rnds = 4" (10 cm) square in the stranded pattern (main body of the hat) using US 10.5 (6.5 mm) needles

Abbreviations

dpns = double-pointed needles

k = knit

k2tog = knit two together

p = purl

rnd(s) = round(s)

st(s) = stitch(es)

Tips to Help You Visualize Your Project and Get You Started

I designed this hat to look like white snow falling against a blue-sky backdrop, but you could totally play with colors to give it a different vibe. Instead of snow falling, it might look like confetti if you used a color combo of deep purple and pink.

As a reminder, you can refer to the Colorwork Basics section (page 9) if you need help with any of the techniques used in this pattern.

PATTERN

Brim

Using US 9 (5.5 mm) circular knitting needles, cast on 60 (72) sts using **Color A**. Place a stitch marker and join in the round.

Rnds 1–9 (**Color A**): *k1, p1; repeat from * to end.

Body

Please read through all of the following notes before beginning the chart.

Switch to US 10.5 (6.5 mm) circular knitting needles.

Fitted version: Work Chart 1 rounds 10–34 and then move on to the **Crown** section.

Slouchy version: Work Chart 1 rounds 10–34 and then work Chart 2 rounds 35–47 before moving on to the **Crown** section.

Each stitch shown in both charts is a knit stitch. Each section of 12 stitches is repeated 5 (6) times per round.

I ended up carrying up my yarn throughout this hat to minimize the number of ends I had to weave in. You can do this by wrapping **Color B** (your working yarn) counterclockwise once around **Color A** (your unused yarn) and then continuing to work the chart. I will indicate these spots on the chart as a friendly reminder!

Fitted version: Cut **Color A** after you complete round 33.

Slouchy version: Cut **Color A** after you complete round 43.

Snowfall Chart 1

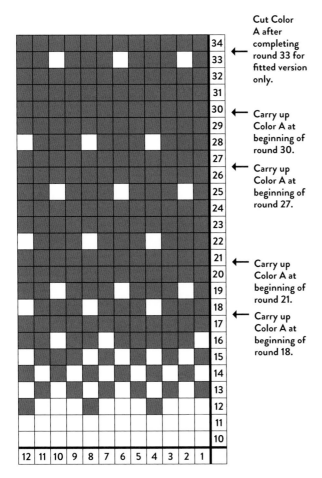

34 ← Cut Color A after completing round 33 for fitted version only.

30 ← Carry up Color A at beginning of round 30.

27 ← Carry up Color A at beginning of round 27.

21 ← Carry up Color A at beginning of round 21.

18 ← Carry up Color A at beginning of round 18.

Snowfall Chart 2

Fitted version: Your hat should measure about 7.5" (19 cm) from the cast-on edge after you complete round 34. If it does not, continue to knit in the round using **Color B** until it does.

Slouchy version: Your hat should measure about 9" (23 cm) from the cast-on edge after you complete round 47. If it does not, continue knitting in the round using **Color B** until it does.

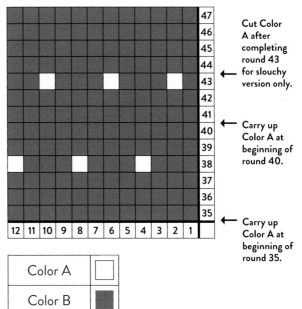

47 ← Cut Color A after completing round 43 for slouchy version only.

40 ← Carry up Color A at beginning of round 40.

35 ← Carry up Color A at beginning of round 35.

| Color A | ☐ |
| Color B | ■ |

Crown

Switch to dpns or Magic Loop method (page 165) when your stitches become too tight on your needles.

Use **Color B** for all remaining rounds.

Rnd 35 (48): *k4, k2tog; repeat from * to end. [50 (60) sts]

Rnd 36 (49): k to end.

Rnd 37 (50): *k3, k2tog; repeat from * to end. [40 (48) sts]

Rnd 38 (51): k to end.

Rnd 39 (52): *k2, k2tog; repeat from * to end. [30 (36) sts]

Rnd 40 (53): k to end.

Rnd 41 (54): *k1, k2tog; repeat from * to end. [20 (24) sts]

Rnd 42 (55): k to end.

Rnd 43 (56): *k2tog; repeat from * to end. [10 (12) sts]

Finishing

Cut **Color B**, making sure to leave a tail about 12" (30 cm) long. Thread the tail through a tapestry needle and then weave it through the live stitches to take your work off your needles. Pull the tail tightly to close the top of your hat.

Weave in all remaining ends.

Feel free to block your hat.

JOY

Starting with a fun, corrugated rib brim with stripes that continue into the body of the hat, this design is packed with elongated stars and little diamonds near the crown to let your spirit shine. You can knit this baby in traditional holiday colors to celebrate the magic of the season, or you can totally switch up your palette and find joy any time of the year! There also are options to create a scrappy version—just play around with whatever yarn you have in your stash to create a one-of-a-kind beauty for yourself or as a gift!

Construction

This hat is worked in the round seamlessly from the brim to the crown.

Size

One size. See the Finished Measurements section on page 155.

This hat is designed for an adult head measuring up to 22" (55 cm). If you do not meet gauge in the stranded pattern (main body of the hat) with the suggested needles, change your needle size to meet gauge and ensure you achieve the right fit. Sizing also can be adjusted by increasing or decreasing the number of cast-on stitches in multiples of 6. Any modification will affect the amount of yarn used.

Materials

Yarn

Approximately 188 yds (172 m) total of worsted weight yarn in four or more contrasting colors

Color A: 42 yds (39 m)

Color B: 47 yds (43 m)

Color C: 70 yds (65 m)

Color D: 29 yds (27 m)

Shown In

Malabrigo Yarn Worsted (100% Merino wool), 210 yds (192 m) per 3.5 oz (100 g)

Color A: Verde Adriana

Color B: Ravelry Red

Color C: Natural

Color D: Frank Ochre

I knit my sample using only four colors, but you can make a scrappy version using a different color for the elongated stars, additional colors for each zigzag, and even new colors for each little diamond and dot near the crown. Any modification will affect the amount of yarn used. The section with the elongated stars and the dots next to them requires roughly 10 yds (10 m). Each zigzag requires roughly 10 yds (10 m). Each section with the diamonds after the zigzags requires about 5 yds (5 m). Each round with dots near the crown requires roughly 2 yds (2 m).

Recommended Yarn Substitution

Lion Brand Yarn Wool-Ease (80% acrylic, 20% wool), 197 yds (180 m) per 3 oz (85 g)

Suggested Needles

US 7 (4.5 mm) 16" (40 cm) circular knitting needles, or size needed to meet gauge

US 9 (5.5 mm) 16" (40 cm) circular knitting needles, or size needed to meet gauge

US 9 (5.5 mm) double-pointed needles or US 9 (5.5 mm) circular knitting needles with a longer cord for Magic Loop method (page 165), or size needed to meet gauge

Notions

Scissors

Stitch marker

Tapestry needle

Finished Measurements

Circumference: 18.75" (47 cm)

Height: 9.25" (23 cm)

Gauge

20.5 sts = 4" (10 cm) and 8 rnds = 1.5" (4 cm) in 1 x 1 ribbing (unstretched) using US 7 (4.5 mm) needles

18 sts x 22 rnds = 4" (10 cm) square in the stranded pattern (main body of the hat) using US 9 (5.5 mm) needles

Abbreviations

dpns = double-pointed needles

k = knit

k2tog = knit two together

p = purl

rnd(s) = round(s)

st(s) = stitch(es)

Tips to Help You Visualize Your Project and Get You Started

This is such a fun knit with so many color combinations that will completely change the vibe depending on your choices! I recommend first choosing the two colors you will use for the corrugated brim (Color A and Color B). Then, I'd suggest picking your background color (Color C) that has a high contrast from your first two colors. Last, I'd choose a Color D that really pops against your background color. It's totally up to you!

As a reminder, you can refer to the Colorwork Basics section (page 9) if you need help with any of the techniques used in this pattern.

PATTERN

Brim

Using US 7 (4.5 mm) circular knitting needles, cast on 84 sts using **Color A**. Place a stitch marker and join in the round.

Rnds 1–8: *k1 (**Color B**), p1 (**Color A**); repeat from * to end.

Cut **Color A**.

Body

Please read through all of the following notes before beginning the chart.

Switch to US 9 (5.5 mm) circular knitting needles and follow the chart, working rounds 9–43.

All stitches shown in the chart are knit stitches. Each section of 6 stitches is repeated 14 times per round.

I have an easy trick to help erase the jogs in your zigzags that I have outlined in the Techniques Section (page 164) at the end of this book. If you'd like to use this trick, you will want to start each round in which a zigzag begins with a new strand of whatever yarn is worked next. If you knit your hat following my sample, you already begin rounds 22 and 25 with new strands of yarn, so that's awesome. To also minimize the appearance of a jog in your first zigzag (if you use the same color for the elongated stars and the first zigzag as I did in my sample), cut **Color D** after completing round 18 and start with a new strand of **Color D** in round 19. This spot will be indicated on the chart as a friendly reminder. Do not weave in your ends until you complete your hat if you choose to use this method.

You also can minimize a jog at the join in a couple of the little diamond shapes near the crown with a simple trick. Knit **only the very last stitch** of round 30 in **Color A**. Then, in round 31, knit **only the very last stitch** of the round in **Color C**. Next, knit **only the very last stitch** of round 36 in **Color D**. Then, in round 37, knit **only the very last stitch** of the round in **Color C**. These places will be indicated on the chart.

In addition, in rounds 40 and 42 you will want to carry up **Color D** (if you use the same color for the dots as I did in my sample). You can do this by wrapping **Color C** (your working yarn) counterclockwise once around **Color D** (your unused yarn) at the beginning of each of those rounds and then continuing to work the chart. These spots will be indicated on the chart.

In general, I cut my colors after each section in which I used them. I will indicate where I cut my colors on the chart. As always, use whatever method works best for you!

If you choose to use a different color than **Color D** for the first zigzag in the pattern, you will be working with three colors in round 19. If you choose to use a different color than **Color A** for the first little diamond shape after the zigzags, you will be working with three colors in round 30. Make sure to maintain your yarn position for each of the three colors as you work those rounds.

Joy Chart

Your hat should measure about 8" (20 cm) from the cast-on edge after completing the chart. If it does not, or if you prefer a bit more slouch, you can continue knitting in the round with **Color C** until you reach that measurement/your desired height before moving on to the **Crown** section. Any modification will affect the amount of yarn used.

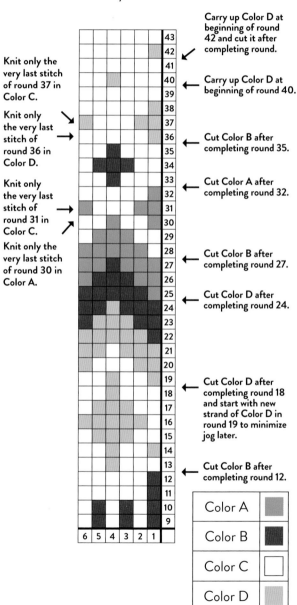

Knit only the very last stitch of round 37 in Color C.

Knit only the very last stitch of round 36 in Color D.

Knit only the very last stitch of round 31 in Color C.

Knit only the very last stitch of round 30 in Color A.

Carry up Color D at beginning of round 42 and cut it after completing round.

Carry up Color D at beginning of round 40.

Cut Color B after completing round 35.

Cut Color A after completing round 32.

Cut Color B after completing round 27.

Cut Color D after completing round 24.

Cut Color D after completing round 18 and start with new strand of Color D in round 19 to minimize jog later.

Cut Color B after completing round 12.

Color A	
Color B	
Color C	
Color D	

Crown

Switch to dpns or Magic Loop method (page 165) when your stitches become too tight on your needles.

Use **Color C** for all remaining rounds.

Rnd 44: *k4, k2tog; repeat from * to end. [70 sts]

Rnd 45: k to end.

Rnd 46: *k3, k2tog; repeat from * to end. [56 sts]

Rnd 47: k to end.

Rnd 48: *k2, k2tog; repeat from * to end. [42 sts]

Rnd 49: k to end.

Rnd 50: *k1, k2tog; repeat from * to end. [28 sts]

Rnd 51: k to end.

Rnd 52: *k2tog; repeat from * to end. [14 sts]

Finishing

Cut **Color C**, making sure to leave a tail about 12" (30 cm) long. Thread the tail through a tapestry needle and then weave it through the live stitches to take your work off your needles. Pull the tail tightly to close the top of your hat.

Weave in all remaining ends.

I recommend steam blocking this hat to smooth out your floats.

QUEEN OF HEARTS

I designed this hat to be a fun accessory for Valentine's Day, or really any day you want to feel like a queen, which should be every day, right? It features a cozy, folded brim to give you an extra layer of warmth. You can choose to go with traditional pinks and purples and use a golden color for the crown, or go neutral with contrasting shades of black, white and gray with a couple pops of color. Choose whatever color combo makes you royally happy!

Construction

This hat is worked in the round seamlessly from the brim to the crown.

Size

One size. See the Finished Measurements section on page 161.

This hat is designed for an adult head measuring up to 22" (55 cm). If you do not meet gauge in the stranded pattern (main body of the hat) with the suggested needles, change your needle size to meet gauge and ensure you achieve the right fit.

Materials

Yarn

Approximately 163 yds (150 m) total of worsted weight yarn in five contrasting colors

Color A: 97 yds (89 m)

Color B: 23 yds (21 m)

Color C: 26 yds (24 m)

Color D: 10 yds (10 m)

Color E: 7 yds (7 m)

Shown In

Mitchell's Creations Bayou (100% superwash Merino wool), 218 yds (199 m) per 3.5 oz (100 g)

Color A: Yin

Color B: Nude-gat

Color C: Desert Rose

Color D: Bordeaux

Color E: Find a Penny

Recommended Yarn Substitutions

Malabrigo Yarn Rios (100% superwash Merino wool), 210 yds (192 m) per 3.5 oz (100 g)

Lion Brand Yarn Basic Stitch Anti-Pilling (100% acrylic), 185 yds (170 m) per 3.5 oz (100 g)

Suggested Needles

US 7 (4.5 mm) 16" (40 cm) circular knitting needles, or size needed to meet gauge

US 8 (5 mm) 16" (40 cm) circular knitting needles, or size needed to meet gauge

US 8 (5 mm) double-pointed needles or US 8 (5 mm) circular knitting needles with a longer cord for Magic Loop method (page 165), or size needed to meet gauge

Notions

Scissors

Stitch marker

Tapestry needle

Finished Measurements

Circumference: 17.75" (44 cm)

Height (from the bottom of the folded brim): 9.75" (24 cm)

Gauge

23 sts x 26 rnds = 4" (10 cm) square in 1 x 1 ribbing (unstretched) using US 7 (4.5 mm) needles

19 sts x 23 rnds = 4" (10 cm) square in the stranded pattern (main body of the hat) using US 8 (5 mm) needles

Abbreviations

dpns = double-pointed needles

k = knit

k2tog = knit two together

p = purl

rnd(s) = round(s)

st(s) = stitch(es)

Tips to Help You Visualize Your Project and Get You Started

*For this pattern, I recommend first choosing the colors you want to use for your hearts (**Color D**) and crowns (**Color E**) and then picking a high contrast color for the background (**Color C**) to make those design elements really pop. **Color A** also plays a large role in this hat, as it's used for the wide, folded brim and parts of the crown, so you could choose this color next. When you pick **Color B**, just make sure it has a good contrast with **Color A**. As always, I find it helpful to lay out all my yarn choices next to each other and play around with them until I get a combo that works best.*

As a reminder, you can refer to the Colorwork Basics section (page 9) if you need help with any of the techniques used in this pattern.

PATTERN

Brim

Using US 7 (4.5 mm) circular knitting needles, cast on 84 sts using **Color A**. Place a stitch marker and join in the round.

Rnds 1–39 (**Color A**): *k1, p1; repeat from * to end.

Your brim should measure roughly 6" (15 cm) from the cast-on edge at this point, resulting in a 3" (8 cm) folded brim. If it does not, just keep repeating the 1 x 1 rib pattern until it does.

Body

Please read through all of the following notes before beginning the chart.

Switch to US 8 (5 mm) circular knitting needles and follow the chart, working rounds 40–69.

All stitches shown in the chart are knit stitches. Each section of 12 stitches is repeated 7 times per round.

To help minimize a jog at the join in the little diamond shape near the bottom of the heart, knit all the stitches in round 46 according to the chart until you get to the very last stitch of the round. Knit **only the very last stitch** of round 46 in **Color D**. Then, in round 47, knit **only the very last stitch** of the round in **Color C**. This will be indicated on the chart as a friendly reminder.

Also, as you knit the hat, there will be some spots where you will want to catch long floats. You can do this by floating the unused color, making sure to leave plenty of slack. Then, on the next round, when you reach the middle of the long float, pick it up with your left needle and knit it together with the next stitch. These spots will be indicated on the chart.

In addition, there will be spots where you will want to carry up **Color A** and **Color B** to avoid having more tails to weave in at the end. You can do this by wrapping your working yarn counterclockwise once around your unused yarn and then continuing to work the chart. These spots will be indicated on the chart.

You also may want to minimize the appearance of jogs in your stripes in rounds 66–69 by following the steps below (see page 164 for more on jogs):

Knit your first round of stripes using **Color A** as called for in the chart. Once you reach the end of the round, remove your stitch marker. Insert your right needle purl-wise into the right leg of the **Color C** stitch below the first **Color A** stitch on your left needle. Then, using your right needle, move that **Color C** stitch up onto your left needle so it is next to the **Color A** stitch. Knit those two stitches together. Replace your stitch marker. This will shift the beginning of your round to the left by one stitch and that is totally okay! (In subsequent rounds, **Color C** will be replaced by **Color B** as you work through the stripes.)

Knit your next round of stripes in **Color B** as called for in the chart. Once you reach the end of the round, remove your stitch marker. Insert your right needle purl-wise into the right leg of the **Color A** stitch below the first **Color B** stitch on your left needle. Then, using your right needle, move that **Color A** stitch up onto your left needle so it is next to the **Color B** stitch. Knit those two stitches together. Replace your stitch marker. Again, the beginning of your round will shift to the left by one stitch, and this is okay!

Repeat both steps as you work through the stripes on the crown.

I cut **Color B** after completing round 42 and not again until I completed the hat. I cut **Color A** after completing round 45 and a final time after completing round 68. I cut **Color C** after completing round 59 and a final time after completing round 65. I cut **Color D** after completing round 52. I cut **Color E** after completing round 57. These spots will be indicated on the chart for you. As always, use whatever method works best for you.

Queen of Hearts Chart

Your hat should measure about 8.25" (21 cm) from the bottom of the folded brim after finishing the chart. If it does not, or if you would prefer a bit more slouch, continue knitting in the round with **Color B** until you reach your desired length before moving on to the **Crown** section. Any modification will affect the amount of yarn used.

Crown

Switch to dpns or Magic Loop method when your stitches become too tight on your needles.

Use **Color B** for all remaining rounds.

Rnd 70: *k4, k2tog; repeat from * to end. [70 sts]

Rnd 71: k to end.

Rnd 72: *k3, k2tog; repeat from * to end. [56 sts]

Rnd 73: k to end.

Rnd 74: *k2, k2tog; repeat from * to end. [42 sts]

Rnd 75: k to end.

Rnd 76: *k1, k2tog; repeat from * to end. [28 sts]

Rnd 77: k to end.

Rnd 78: *k2tog; repeat from * to end. [14 sts]

Finishing

Cut **Color B**, making sure to leave a tail about 12" (30 cm) long. Thread the tail through a tapestry needle and then weave it through the live stitches to take your work off your needles. Pull the tail tightly to close the top of your hat.

Weave in all remaining ends.

I highly recommend steam blocking this hat to showcase those beautiful hearts and crowns.

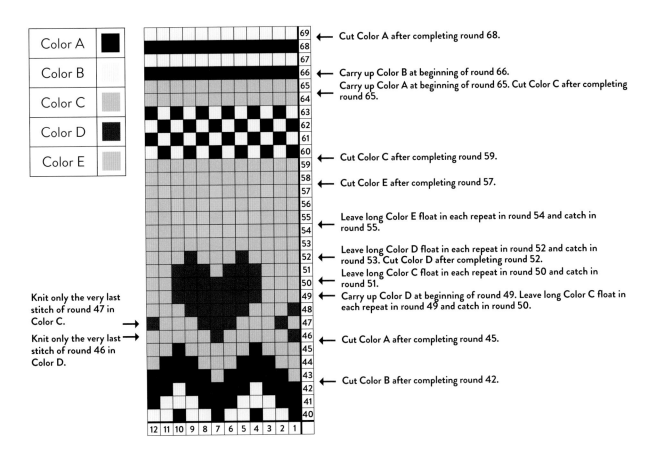

TECHNIQUES

I wanted to share with you some simple tricks and techniques to help with your knitting, my friends!

How to Minimize the Appearance of Jogs in Your Zigzags

This trick works for patterns in this book that involve zigzags. It allows you to use your tails to cover up jogs in the color pattern. Jogs occur when you're knitting in the round because you're essentially knitting in a spiral. So, each round starts stacking on top of the next and that can sometimes result in a jagged look at the join. There are various ways to minimize the appearance of jogs, and this is one way. This technique is done **after** you complete your hat as you're weaving in the ends.

1.   Lay your hat out flat with the side with the join facing up.

2.   Reach inside your hat and find the tail that marks the first stitch of the first zigzag (closest to the brim), and thread the tail from that stitch through a tapestry needle.

3.   Poke your needle through the middle of that first stitch from the inside of your hat, pulling the tail through to the front.

4.   Next, find the closest stitch of the same color located diagonally up to the right on the same zigzag. Poke your needle through the middle of that stitch from the front of your hat, pulling the tail through to the inside of your work. (Do not pull your tail too tightly.)

5.   Then, find the first stitch of the next zigzag, thread the tail from that stitch through a tapestry needle and repeat steps 3 and 4, working your way from brim to crown, until you have covered up all the jogs in your zigzags.

Weave in all remaining ends.

How to Minimize the Appearance of Jogs in Your Single Stripes

In Carousel (page 111), Fall Feels (page 139) and Queen of Hearts (page 159), I used this technique to help minimize the appearance of jogs in my single stripes.

1. Knit your first round of stripes using the color called for in the chart. Once you reach the end of the round, remove your stitch marker.

2. Insert your right needle purl-wise into the right leg of the stitch below the first stitch on your left needle.

3. Then, using your right needle, move that stitch up onto your left needle.

4. Now, knit those two stitches together.

5. Replace your stitch marker. This will shift the beginning of your round to the left by one stitch and that is totally okay!

6. Continue to knit your next round of stripes using the color called for in the chart, repeating steps 1 through 5 as you work each new round of stripes.

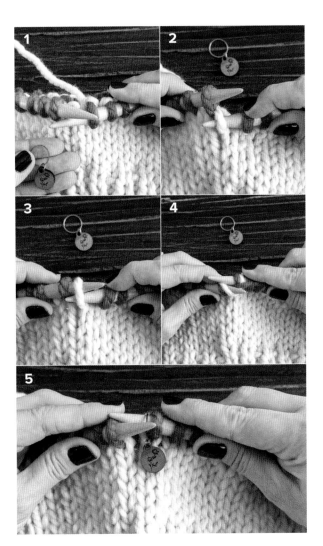

Magic Loop Method

When you're knitting the decrease rounds of the crown of a hat, there comes a point when your stitches begin to feel too tight on your needles—as if they won't comfortably stretch fully around them. This is the time when you can use the Magic Loop method to help you out.

1. At the beginning of a round, switch to a longer cord on your circular needles. All of the hats in this book are knit with 16" (40-cm) circular needles, so you might consider switching to a 24" (60-cm) cord, a 36" (90-cm) cord or longer. The goal is to get more slack with your cord to give you better ease when working your stitches. Use the cord length that works best for you!

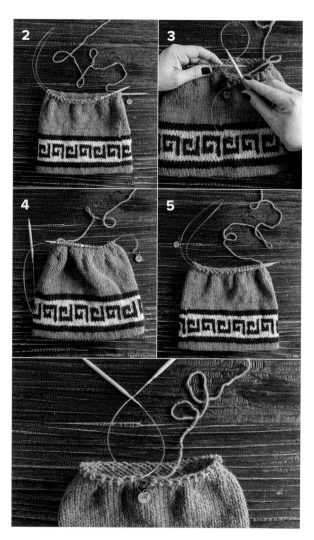

2.   Now, fold your work in half—it doesn't have to be perfect—so it's lying flat in front of you with the needle tips on your right and the cord through the crown of your hat on your left. Pull the middle of the long cord out from the halfway point on the left side of your work so the stitches are divided as evenly as possible on your needle tips and the slack from the long cord remains off to the left side.

3.   Next, pick up your work as if to knit, holding the left needle (the needle that was on top when your work was lying flat) in your left hand and the right needle (the needle that was on the bottom when your work was lying flat) in your right hand. Make sure your stitch marker is on your right needle at the beginning of your round. Now, pull the cord attached to your right needle away from the stitches with the extra slack you have, keeping the stitches on the left needle right where they are.

4.   Knit the stitches on your left needle as usual, according to your pattern, until you reach the end of the half of the stitches you are knitting. If you are working a stitch repeat, keep track of what stitch you are on before you move on to the next step. And if you end up on a k2tog or ssk with only one stitch left on your cord, that's totally okay. Just slide that stitch down your left needle and onto the cord and work the k2tog or ssk when you begin knitting the second half of your stitches in the next step.

5.   Now, fold your work in half again, using your stitch marker as an indicator of the end of the round/ second half. Your hat should be lying flat in front of you with the needle tips on your right and the cord through the crown of your hat on your left. Pull the middle of the long cord out from the second half of your work, making sure the stitches are again divided as evenly as possible on your needle tips and the slack from the long cord remains off to the left side.

6.   Knit the stitches on your left needle as usual, according to your pattern until you reach the end of the round as indicated by your stitch marker.

7.   Repeat steps 2–6, knitting each round according to your pattern, until you complete your hat.

How to Weave in Tails

I get a lot of questions about the best way to weave in tails to make sure the wrong color from a tail doesn't show through on the front of your work. I have tried many different techniques and wanted to share with you the one I find works best. This method is easiest when working with plied yarn, but I also use it when working with single-ply yarns.

1. Turn your hat inside out and lay it flat.

2. Thread the first tail you'd like to weave in through a tapestry needle.

3. Insert the tip of your needle lengthwise through the middle of the plies (or straight through a single ply) of the stitches along the inside of your work and pull through after about 1" (2.5 cm).

4. Now, repeat step 3 going the opposite direction through the stitches right next to where you just weaved in the tail.

5. Cut your tail, leaving just about 0.25" (6 mm).

By weaving tails through the center of the yarn, you minimize the chance of seeing any unwanted color on the right side of your work.

YARN RESOURCES

Big Twist

www.joann.com

Fully Spun

www.fullyspun.com

Jems Luxe Fibers

www.jemsluxefibers.com

Lion Brand Yarn

www.lionbrand.com

Loops & Threads

www.michaels.com

Malabrigo Yarn

www.malabrigoyarn.com

Mitchell's Creations

www.mitchellscreations.com

Mountain Laurel Fiber Co.

www.etsy.com/shop/MtnLaurel-FiberCo

Neighborhood Fiber Co.

www.neighborhoodfiberco.com

OMG Yarn (Balls)

www.etsy.com/shop/omgyarnballs

ACKNOWLEDGMENTS

Thank you to the awesome knitting community for embracing my designs and showing so much love for my crazy color combinations. I want to spread that love by thanking my fellow knitters, crocheters, makers and artists for creating their own unique work that inspires us all to be the best versions of ourselves we can be.

Thank you to the companies and independent dyers that so graciously provided yarn support for this book: Fully Spun; Jems Luxe Fibers; Lion Brand Yarn; Malabrigo Yarn; Mitchell's Creations; Mountain Laurel Fiber Co.; Neighborhood Fiber Co.; and OMG Yarn (Balls). Their gorgeous creations brought each one of my patterns to life.

Thank you to Sarah Walworth, the tech editor who worked with me on this project. She made sure all the patterns in this book are their absolute best, and I thank my lucky stars for her expertise, guidance and support.

Many thanks to Page Street Publishing Co. for giving me this awesome opportunity. And thanks to Caitlin Dow, the editor at Page Street who oversaw this project and helped me navigate through the whole process.

There's no way this book would be a reality without the help of an amazing group of dedicated makers who signed up for this ride with me and enthusiastically tested each and every pattern I sent their way. Thank you to Stephanie Hutchison, Jessica Love, Brianna Callahan, Kimberley Bennett, Barbara Lechtanski, Katie Boyes, Carla Johnson Brown, Danielle Lisle, Christi Mikolas Alexander, Ann Johnston, Mindy Frost, Filippa Caiolino, Tara Taylor, Tami Kaczmarek, Micaela Scott, Tammy Lajeunesse, Fiona Flynn, Mary Stiles, Lynn Campbell, Nat Krayenvenger, Georgie Hutton, Erin Gates, Sandra James, Elaine Smith, Mandi Coffeen, Leigh-Anna Plummer, Sue Bralich, Lesley Johnson, Laura Fox, Christine Beutner and Carla Billingsley.

Thanks to Shannon Loud of Memory Lanes Photography in Richmond, Illinois, for helping me complete the photography for this book with her gorgeous portrait shots. Thank you, also, to the wonderful women (and some of their adorable children) who modeled hats for this book: Danielle Robinson; Channell and Levi Stoby; Erin and Kaitlyn Lett; and Becca Rosati.

Thank you to the awesome group of women who have supported and encouraged me throughout my life and my knitting adventures. Thanks to my very best friend on the planet, Kim Simms, who has been a guiding force in my world since childhood. Much love to my mother-in-law, Ruth Flynn, and my sister-in-law, Liz Knaebe, for their unconditional support. Thank you to Natasha Korecki, Lesley Rogers Krokower and Nancy Landt for always believing in me and my knitting. Thank you to Kristina Paschall for encouraging me to share my knitting on social media in the first place. Thanks to Meredith Price and Jaime Earing for being there for me and reminding me to laugh. Thank you to Erin Gates and Mandi Coffeen for always being in my corner and rooting for me. And thank you to all my friends at Park School in Round Lake, Illinois, who supported me from the very beginning of my knitting journey.

Thank you to my brother and sister-in-law, Brett and Nicole Challos, who have always been there for me no matter what. And thanks to my father-in-law, Dr. Flynn, and my bonus in-laws, Candy and Al Bihlmeier, for all their love.

Thanks to Stephanie Lotven for her generosity, support and encouragement. And thanks to the Richardson family for taking a chance on my knitting from the get-go.

A special thanks to those who made all the pattern photos in this book happen. My awesome neighbor, Amy Larish, has always been super supportive of my knitting and lets me collect flowers and leaves from her yard for my pictures. So many of the colorful blooms found in these pages also came from Mini Earth Greenhouses in Grayslake, Illinois.

And last, but definitely not least, the most heartfelt thank you in the world to my incredibly supportive and encouraging husband, Tim Flynn, who has the patience of a saint and always believes in me and encourages me when I'm not even quite sure myself. Thank you also to my awesome kids, Fiona and Kiefer, for letting me live out my knitting dreams and not complaining too much about Mom having yarn all over the house.

ABOUT THE AUTHOR

Courtney Flynn is a knitwear designer who focuses on creating colorful accessories inspired by art and nature. Her patterns have gained attention for their bold color combinations and versatility by utilizing scrap yarn. She lives in Illinois with her husband, two children and their border collie mix rescue dog, Penny. This is her first knitting book. For more information about her designs and work, please visit www.flynnknit.com.

INDEX